VALUES GROUNDED
PARENTING

VALUES GROUNDED PARENTING

A Framework for Raising Healthy Children

MICHAEL J. REDIVO PH.D.

The content of this book is for informational and educational purposes only. Nothing in this book is intended to be a substitute for professional therapeutic, psychological, psychiatric, or medical advice, diagnosis, or treatment. The activities in the book are designed to help you better understand how to apply parenting principles and not intended to be a substitute for therapeutic, psychological, or psychiatric advice. If in the event you recognize some stress as a result of any material from the book, it is recommended that you seek the help of a trained, licensed mental health professional.

Copyright © 2020 by Michael J. Redivo

All rights reserved. This book, or parts thereof,
may not be reproduced in any form without permission.

Paperback ISBN: 978-1-7343973-0-7
Hardcover ISBN: 978-1-7343973-1-4
E-book ISBN: 978-1-7343973-2-1

Printed in the United States of America

1 3 5 7 9 10 8 6 4 2

This book is dedicated to H.S., my best friend and voice of wisdom and guidance. Your continued prompting and encouragement made this possible.

CONTENTS

INTRODUCTION — 1

PILLAR I: PARENTING WITH VISION, PURPOSE, & POSITIVE VALUES — 8

CHAPTER 1 • Vision: Defining Your Positive Purpose as Parents — 9

CHAPTER 2 • Positive Values: Defining What Defines You — 29

CHAPTER 3 • Family Culture and Your Family Blueprint — 55

PILLAR II: THE FIVE C'S: EFFECTIVE PARENTING STRATEGIES & PRINCIPLES — 74

CHAPTER 4 • Consistency and Competency: Growing Trust and Confidence — 75

CHAPTER 5 • Clarity and Calmness: Maintaining Positive Direction and Mindfulness — 87

CHAPTER 6 • Consequences: Shaping Values Grounded Behavior — 103

PILLAR III: BOUNDARIES, LIMITS, & DISCIPLINE — 124

CHAPTER 7 • Protecting the Pathway toward Growing Up — 125

CHAPTER 8 • Wants versus Needs: An Epic Battle and Growing Pains — 137

CHAPTER 9 • The VPC: Applying Effective Limits and Consequences — 147

CHAPTER 10 • Boundaries, Limits, and Consequences with Technology **161**

CHAPTER 11 • Discipline: Stay Grounded or Be Grounded 171

PILLAR IV: PRODUCTIVE CONFLICT, MISTAKES, AND GROWTH OPPORTUNITIES **200**

CHAPTER 12 • Productive Conflict as a Catalyst for Growth 201

CHAPTER 13 • The Three E's of Productive Conflict 229

CHAPTER 14 • Mistake Making and Mistake Management 245

APPENDICES	**261**
ACKNOWLEDGMENTS	**277**
REFERENCES	**281**
ABOUT THE AUTHOR	**283**
LETTER TO READERS	**285**

INTRODUCTION

ANITA AND HER FAMILY sought counseling because there was too much conflict and arguing at home. Tom, the father, explained that one minute the kids (ages 11, 9, and 6) would get along famously, and the next was like a World Wrestling match, complete with loud thuds, crashes, and screams. One accusing the other of shoving and name calling, escalating into slinging insults at each other. The kids were nearly hypnotized by their electronic devices, and they avoided homework like it was a bad odor. Emotionally charged power struggles erupted when it was time to put away the electronics and take care of their responsibilities. Their family was super busy, and always on the go.

Both parents worked full time. Managing the day-to-day routine seemed like an Olympic event. They were physically and emotionally exhausted by the end of each day and felt defined by their overwhelming circumstances. In efforts to stop the yelling, they yelled. Arguments escalated, typically to the point where either parent made shallow threats. When the kids questioned "why" they had to do what their parents requested, the parents exhorted, "Because I SAID SO!"

INTRODUCTION

Worn out and emotionally drained, the parents were hoping that I could offer some guidance to restore cooperation and respect within their family. They both asked, "How can we get our kids to listen to us and get along with each other? We hate having to yell and argue. It seems they only listen when we yell and threaten punishment!"

Anita and Tom's story reflects a common struggle for many parents. Their parenting approach was in reaction to the circumstances of the day, which were often harried and stressful. As a result, they found themselves being consistently inconsistent with boundaries, limits, and discipline. They were emotionally reactive versus responsive in their day-to-day parenting. Because of the lack of a clear, consistent, and positive direction, the kids were acting out, as most kids would, with behavior that was growing down as opposed to growing up.

During our work together, we identified a clear, positive parenting purpose, also known as a shared vision. The parents defined and created a vision statement that read: *To raise our kids with great values so they will grow into successful adults.* This vision became the centerpiece for everything they did as parents. Next, as a family, they identified a series of positive values that were essential to growing into successful adults. This was followed by highlighting behaviors that demonstrate these values. Tom and Anita then defined their family blueprint, outlining behavior expectations and a day-to-day routine. They pledged to work at being more consistent and united in their co-parenting efforts.

We then examined how they could manage conflict productively. In fact, they discovered conflict was useful for meaningful learning and growth. Of course, as in all families, mistakes were made in their efforts to transform into more of a values grounded family. They used their mistakes as fertilizer to help them grow and learn.

A key part to their work was accepting accountability or ownership for behaving according to their values. As a result, the yelling came to an end. Because everyone was taking accountability and practicing respect, the kids' confidence and self-esteem grew, and the parents no longer felt defined by their overwhelming circumstances.

Their family culture shifted from being defined by stressful circumstances to one that is defined by positive values. Boundaries and limits were much easier to apply as they were no longer punitive, but instead protective. As we finished, the family completed their family culture board and posted it in their home as a declaration of a new, healthier family identity.

Like most parents and families, Tom and Anita realized that positive values were already within them and their kids. What they lacked was a clear framework for developing and building these values within their day-to-day parenting. This book provides that framework for you.

VALUABLE FRAMEWORK

Since it is your role to guide your children, it is important to ask, what is guiding you? If it is your day-to-day stressful circumstances, harried schedule, and exhausted mood, you are not achieving your potential as a parent.

On the other hand, if you are guided and defined by a strong purpose and positive values, you become visionary as parents. The values grounded framework is designed to grow your positive values within your household, creating a solid and anchored family culture. This not only strengthens your confidence as a parent, but also that of your children.

This book offers an effective framework for how to define and carry out your role as a values grounded parent. If you believe that consistent

INTRODUCTION

practice of positive values is key to raising healthy and well-behaved children, this book is for you. If you believe that it is your job as a parent to create a positive family culture that helps everyone at home learn, grow, and thrive, this book is for you. Whether you are new to parenting or seasoned veterans, this book will help you raise responsible children who are ready to take on the real world.

The Values Grounded framework serves as a foundation for parents and children of all ages. Whether you are a two parent family, a single parent family, a blended family or a foster family, this unique approach will help you cultivate a healthy home environment to raise your beautiful children.

THE FOUR PILLARS OF THE VALUES GROUNDED FRAMEWORK

So, how does one become a values grounded parent? There are Four Pillars that are detailed in the following chapters.

PILLAR I: VISION, PURPOSE, & POSITIVE VALUES

The first step is establishing your vision or positive purpose as a parent. Your vision serves as your parenting compass, providing direction and guidance. The next step is to define your positive values. These values help you accomplish your vision. Once your vision and values are clarified, the following step is to design your family blueprint. This provides helpful structure for day-to-day happenings within your family. Together, each of the above steps serves to cultivate your family culture. The culture within your home reflects your strength as a family. As part of being a values grounded parent, it is good practice to document your family culture on a "culture board." The activity in Chapter 3 will guide you and your family through the steps to create your "One-of-a-Kind Family Culture Board."

PILLAR II: PRACTICING THE 5 C'S

The 5 C's reflect best practices in parenting. These are research-based strategies that will help increase your confidence and effectiveness as a values grounded parent. Consistency, Calmness, Competency, Clarity, and Consequences are the principles that serve to strengthen your day-to-day parenting efforts to keep your family culture strong and values grounded.

PILLAR III: BOUNDARIES, LIMITS, AND DISCIPLINE

Applying effective boundaries, limits, and consequences is key to reinforcing positive behavior with your children AND protecting the integrity of your family culture. Disciplining is an important part of this process. Values grounded disciplining is a positive, yet firm approach designed to help your children correct their ungrounded or negative behavior without the blame or shame.

PILLAR IV: PRODUCTIVE CONFLICT, MISTAKES, AND GROWTH OPPORTUNITIES

In their efforts to grow up, children make many, many mistakes … as do their parents. Mistake making is a common, yet important part in growing together as a family. This framework will teach you and your children to use conflict and mistakes as fertile opportunities to learn and grow. This creates a home environment that fosters trust and positive intimacy.

Each of the Pillars builds upon the others. By aligning your day-to-day parenting in accordance with the 4 Pillars, you protect the integrity of your values and culture that ultimately define you as a family.

INTRODUCTION

Although your circumstances as a family will change over time, the Pillars ensure that your values and family culture remain constant—guiding you through the various seasons of your life.

HOW TO USE THIS BOOK

The focus throughout the book is on ***real-world application***. Therefore, each concept is explained and then followed by real-world examples, activities, and practical suggestions. It is recommend that you read the book through in sequence. This will help you get a clear understanding of the framework and how it can work for you and your family. Since there is a lot of content, you can then bounce around from chapter to chapter, using it as a reference as needed.

Specific examples, practical tips, and guidelines are provided throughout, especially in the chapters on discipline, boundaries, limits, consequences, and productive conflict. Specific guidance around discipline, parent-child dialogue, and conflict resolution is provided. The examples help you see what these concepts actually sound and look like in real world examples. You can take the information from these examples and practical tips and suggestions and apply them right away with your kids.

In order to be a values grounded parent, it is important to be involved and active. Therefore, within each chapter, there are activities to help you engage the ideas, concepts, and principles. Through active participation, you will find that you develop a deeper and more personally meaningful understanding of key values grounded concepts and principles.

It is recommended that you complete these activities with your spouse or co-parent. If you are a single parent, consider discussing your responses with a family member or a close friend who knows your children.

VALUES GROUNDED PARENTING

All examples come from real-world situations. Names and identifying information of those involved have been altered to protect their privacy and confidentiality.

As a clinical psychologist specializing in work with parents and children for more than 20 years, I am humbled by the complexity of the human condition and the multitude of challenges parents face. I have learned firsthand that effective parenting involves on-the-job learning. The notion of perfect parenting simply does not exist nor does raising perfect kids.

Over the years, I have been amazed, humbled, and inspired by the many stories parents have shared with me in their efforts to raise their children. As a husband of 25 years and a father of two beautiful children, I have felt similarly about our efforts.

At the urging of family, friends, clients, and colleagues, I have shared my professional and personal experiences and knowledge in the pages that follow. The key concepts are informed by best practices in parenting and supported by decades of clinical research. It is my hope that you will join other values grounded parents in using this effective framework in raising your kids as well as growing confidence and joy as a parent.

PILLAR I
PARENTING WITH VISION, PURPOSE, & POSITIVE VALUES

CHAPTER 1

VISION: DEFINING YOUR POSITIVE PURPOSE AS PARENTS

"Why do I have to do my homework now? I am in the middle of a game."

"WHY am I in trouble? HE'S the one who started it!"

"None of my friends have THESE rules. This makes NO sense . . . Why are you SO unfair!"

"Why do YOU have to meet my friends? Don't you trust me?"

"I wanna play . . . why do I have to get ready for bed now?"

DOES THIS SOUND familiar? Children often question and protest their parent's efforts at teaching responsibility and other values grounded behaviors.

For many parents, their response to their kids' questions is a resounding, "Because I SAID SO!" Often times, this is out of frustration. Underlying their questions, however, children are seeking direction and leadership from their parents.

Raising healthy values grounded children starts with accepting your role as a leader in your family. Your children need you to

CHAPTER 1: VISION

lead and guide them. Effective leadership is driven by a positive vision and not one's ego. Vision has to do with the bigger picture or purpose behind your day-to-day parenting. This purpose provides meaningful and positive answers to the litany of "why" and "how come" questions.

In this chapter, your parenting vision and purpose will be examined and clarified. This will help you guide and lead your children effectively. Without a vision, you are prone to parenting based on your circumstances and emotion, making you a reactive and inconsistent leader. A strong vision helps anchor your day-to-day parenting so it remains consistent with your positive purpose.

As you take your first step in developing your vision, it is important to know that effective leaders are by no means perfect. Parenting involves on-the-job learning. With a strong vision, you establish a positive standard from which to pursue and correct your course as needed.

BECOMING A VISIONARY PARENT

Your vision is your long-term, positive goal as parents. It is the centerpiece for what you are hoping to accomplish in raising your children. It connects your day-to-day parenting with an overall goal or bigger picture. It is the "why" behind what you say and do as parents.

Since it is your job to guide your children, it is important to ask, what is guiding you? Your vision provides this guide. It offers direction so you can manage the day-to-day responsibilities and challenges of parenting without losing sight of your long-term, positive goal. Your kids regularly seek direction from you and need to know why you guide and direct them the way you do.

VALUES GROUNDED PARENTING

Let's look at a few brief examples of how a vision informs day-to-day parenting decisions and actions. Let's say Mr. and Mrs. Jones have the following vision (overall long-term, positive goal):

Our purpose as parents is to help our children grow up in a loving and healthy way with positive values.

When their kids protest doing homework, the parents fall back on their vision and remind the kids that it is very hard to grow up without a solid education. Since their overall goal or vision is to help them grow up in a healthy and loving way, they ensure that their kids complete their schoolwork.

When the kids want to have Hot Cheetos and ice cream for lunch, the parents fall back on their vision and remind the kids that a balanced, nutritious lunch provides necessary fuel to grow and learn. Therefore, balanced nutrition is reinforced as part of maintaining their vision.

When the kids argue and sling nasty words at each other, the parents redirect the kids and apply consequences to teach them the importance of handling conflict in respectful ways. The parents use their vision to help their kids see that handling conflict and difficult emotion respectfully is essential to growing up in healthy and loving ways.

When the kids are playing cooperatively and respectfully, the parents fall back on their vision and provide praise, reinforcing that cooperation strengthens relationships, which is an important part of growing up.

YOUR VISION SERVES TO PROTECT

Your vision establishes you as a leader in your family and serves a protective role. It protects you from losing sight of your positive purpose as a parent. For most parents, their day-to-day parenting challenges can easily blind them their sense of purpose. When you lose sight (pun

CHAPTER 1: VISION

intended) of your vision, you are more prone to being overwhelmed and behaving in reactive ways with your kids.

Your vision helps you rise above your day-to-day challenges and the shifting moods that come along with them. It leads you to a higher ground and reminds you to behave in ways that are consistent with how you want to raise your kids as opposed to simply overreacting to stressful circumstances. The following example illustrates this.

DEFINED BY YOUR VISION... OR YOUR CIRCUMSTANCES?

The Williams family were close knit. Johnny and Adam (ages 10 and 8, respectively) were daredevil type brothers. They did stunt jumping on their bikes and amazing tricks on their skateboards. Both kids suffered from severe allergies. They were allergic to washing dishes, cleaning their room, homework, and vegetables. Mr. and Mrs. Williams were hardworking parents, doing their best to raise their boys.

Johnny had a volcanic temper. When he got upset, he would say things that would make a sailor blush, especially when told to get off the computer. Setting limits on gaming was a huge trigger. In these moments, the parents did their best to try and calm Johnny. After their unsuccessful attempts, the parents would lose it and the temper became contagious. Additionally, Johnny's relationship with his brother was being affected—Adam started to become fearful of his older brother.

The parents felt lost and at wit's end with their wonderful, yet combustible son. They also felt that they were being more and more defined by their negative circumstances as opposed to a more positive vision. Although interested in the idea, the parents did not have a shared vision for raising their daredevil sons.

VALUES GROUNDED PARENTING

Exploring their overall, positive goal and purpose as parents helped them loosen the grip of being defined by negative circumstances and snarky emotions. The parents developed the following vision: *To raise our boys with character and positive values so they grow into successful young men.*

With this vision, the parents became more empowered with a positive focus. They shared the vision with their boys and explained that everything they do as parents will be related to this vision.

Both boys appreciated and supported the vision. However, they did not like the idea that limiting screen time was part of helping them develop character and positive values. As most kids do, they questioned their parents' actions. Specifically, they wondered how decreasing gaming was related to growing into young men of character and value.

Sticking to their vision, the parents Googled the hazards and addictive nature of gaming and social media. As a family, they read and discussed this topic. The boys learned, much to their surprise, the addictive nature of social media and gaming. In fact, they also learned many of the game developers in Silicon Valley have very strict limits in their families around screen use!

As a result of connecting their positive vision to their day-to-day parenting, the issue of screen time was addressed in a respectful and reasonable manner. The boys understood the limit much better and it made sense. They accepted it, but *still thought it stunk.* The parents praised their kids' emerging maturity, noting that doing what is right and healthy is not always easy.

Next, the parents challenged Johnny to manage his anger and temper in ways that would help him grow into a successful young man (vision). When he followed rules and managed his emotions well, he received a great deal of positive feedback (praise and earning rewards). When he reacted in disrespectful ways, his parents calmly used

CHAPTER 1: VISION

discipline and consequences (suspending computer time, grounding to his room) to teach Johnny the value of practicing anger management. While grounded to his room, his parents requested that he write a paragraph on how handling anger in respectful ways (day-to-day actions) will help him grow into a successful young man (vision).

Over time, Johnny learned important skills in managing anger, frustration, and disappointment. He also learned that it was his job to deal with his anger as opposed to relying on his parents to "not make him mad."

I talked with the family about how growing into a young man of character is not always easy. There are various stressors and challenges along the way—we called these "growing pains." However, with a clearly defined vision, they are far better prepared to manage such growing pains and minimize the drama that ensnared them.

The above example illustrates how a vision keeps you on track toward a positive, long-term, parenting goal. Without it, you can get caught up in unproductive power struggles, and being led by reactive emotion. This example also illustrates the importance of sharing your vision with your kids. This helps them understand the reason why you parent the way you do.

The first step is to establish a vision for your parenting.

So, how do you develop a vision and what does one look like? Well, for starters, let's begin with some thought and reflection about your purpose as parents. The following activity will help guide you in better understanding and clarifying your purpose:

ACTIVITY: WHAT'S YOUR PURPOSE?

Write down your thoughts and responses to the following questions:

- What am I hoping to accomplish as a parent? What is my overall, long-term, positive goal?
- What is my purpose in being a parent?
- What were my parents hoping to accomplish when raising me? If possible, ask your parent(s) this question.
- If I were to ask my kids what they think my purpose as a parent is, what would they say?
- How often do I think about my parenting purpose? If I thought about my parenting purpose more often, how might this influence how I interact with my children?

As indicated in the introduction, discuss your responses with your spouse/partner. If you are a single parent, discuss your responses with a trusted adult who knows your family. As you discuss and share, be sure to be open-minded and avoid judgment.

Hopefully, this activity helped clarify and refine your sense of purpose as a parent. For some of you, this may have been the first time you ever thought directly about your parenting purpose. Remember that effective leadership is fueled by a clearly defined, positive purpose.

CHAPTER 1: VISION

The next step is to capture your parenting purpose in a vision statement. However, before doing so, let's explore the value of a united front among parents.

THE UNITED FRONT

As you read the following two examples, put yourself in the place of the sailor who is seeking answers from the co-captains.

EXAMPLE 1:
The USS Growth *has set sail on a routine trip. As they depart, a curious sailor makes her way up to the bridge and asks both co-captains, "Where are we headed?" One co-captain responds, "Well, we are headed to the Unified Coast, where we will dock and explore new territory." The other co-captain chimes in, "Indeed, it will be an exciting journey with challenges along the way!" They both remind the sailor, "Please ensure that the decks are clean and the galley prepared for mealtime."*

EXAMPLE 2:
The USS Ego *has set sail on a routine trip. As they depart, a curious sailor makes his way up to the bridge and asks the co-captains, "Where are we headed?" One co-captain announces, "We are headed due north toward the Divided Islands." Abruptly, the other co-captain interrupts, "Heck NO! There is no way we are heading there! We are heading due east toward the Self-Centered Coast." They begin to argue, one trying to talk over the other. Each co-captain tries to convince the sailor that the other does not know what the heck they are doing. The co-captains get lost in their own ego-driven argument. They don't even recognize that the sailor left the bridge.*

VALUES GROUNDED PARENTING

What was your experience of being the sailor in Example 1? Pay attention to your feelings and thoughts. What impact did the unity and clarity regarding the direction of the ship have on your feelings and thoughts? How safe and secure did you feel on the *USS Growth*? Describe your trust of the co-captains.

Now, let's switch to Example 2. What was your experience of being the sailor? Pay attention to your feelings and thoughts. What impact did the lack of unity and clarity regarding the direction of the ship have on your feelings and thoughts? How safe and secure did you feel on the *USS Ego*? Describe your trust of the co-captains.

As you have probably guessed, the above examples are symbolic of co-parenting—the degree to which both parents work together in raising their children. If the co-captains/co-parents are united in their vision, the children or sailors are clear and secure about the direction they are being led. The expectations within the family or on the ship are clear. With such clarity and consistency, expectations or family rules are much more likely to be followed.

Conversely, if co-parents are divided in their vision, conflict mounts about which direction to steer or guide their family. The children become stressed and begin to distrust their parents' ability to safely lead them. The lack of unity and direction combined with inconsistencies invokes anxiety for all involved. It is a universal need to know what direction one is being led. Without a shared and united direction, children become rather confused and anxious, AND less likely to follow parental direction.

Furthermore, a united front among co-parents provides the necessary support to manage challenging life circumstances along your journey. Stormy seas, bad weather, problems with the ship can be handled much better when there is a united front amongst the co-parents. This unity bolsters support and strength to withstand tough challenges along your journey so you get to your intended destination—raising your children into values grounded young adults.

CHAPTER 1: VISION

UNITY AND SECURITY

Children need to feel secure and safe in order to learn, grow, and thrive. Their experience of security enables them to go out of their comfort zone, take appropriate risks, and discover positive ways to engage life. Additionally, when your children feel secure, they are more likely to trust your vision and follow your direction and guidance.

When it comes to boundaries, limits, and discipline, a united front is a must. As described later, most kids often experience limits, boundaries, and negative consequences as a form of rejection and try to avoid them. If you are united in your vision, you strengthen your boundaries and discipline. This makes limit setting and consequences more effective with far less drama. On the other hand, if you are not unified in your vision, your kids can play you against one another, diluting the effectiveness of limit setting and creating unnecessary drama and overreactions.

UNITED FRONT AND STYLISTIC DIFFERENCES

Maintaining a united front does not mean that co-parents ought to be clones of one another. Rather, the united front is a stance where you agree on your shared vision and positive values that support and fortify your family culture. It means you back each other up and support one another, especially in *front* of the children. As in most co-parenting relationships, both parents will have stylistic differences in how to relate to the kids. The united front does not have to take away these differences. Rather, it serves to enhance them.

So, what is meant by stylistic differences? This relates to your parenting style, which is informed by various personality traits and the parenting you experienced when growing up. These traits influence how you relate to your spouse/partner, your children, and others. They shape and guide your relationships. Parenting styles have been studied and documented extensively over the years. It is important for you to understand your unique attributes and style as co-parents.

The following activity will help you gain greater understanding and appreciation for you and your co-parent's parenting style:

ACTIVITY: WHAT'S YOUR STYLE?

Write down your thoughts and responses to the following questions:

- Think about three positives of both you and your partner's parenting style. Take some scratch paper and write each positive on a separate piece of paper, fold it in half, and put it in a bag. Be sure to indicate if the positive is yours or your partners. Next, following the same directions, write down three areas of improvement for you and your partner with regard to parenting style and put these in the bag. For single parents, do this activity with a trusted adult(s). Ask them to write positives of your parenting style and areas to improve.
- Take turns picking out and discussing one piece at a time.
- Next, discuss how you can support the other's unique style in your day-to-day parenting routine.
- As you have this conversation, be mindful to not be judgmental or sarcastic. Remember, if you want your co-parent to be open to feedback, you must be open to feedback as well. By identifying certain skills that you can improve as a parent, you open the door for improvement and growth.

CHAPTER 1: VISION

This activity is important on two levels. First, the *content* opens up dialogue for you and your co-parent to learn more about each other. Second, the *process* invites you as co-parents to engage one another in meaningful conversation. Using the earlier example, co-captains are far more successful at guiding their team of sailors when they are involved in ongoing communication.

Most of the time, parents engage each other on transactional matters such as clarifying the kids' school schedules, getting them to soccer, planning birthday parties, and so on. What oftentimes gets neglected are discussions on parenting purpose, parenting styles, and how best to support one another. In my work as a family therapist and my day-to-day walk as a father, I have noticed that once parents begin to have productive conversations about their styles and ways to be more united in their parenting, they become more effective, intimacy is enhanced, and confidence grows—not only for the parents but also within their kids.

So, now that you have examined your parenting purpose and the importance of maintaining a united front, you are ready to develop a shared vision.

SHARED VISION FOR PARENTING

A shared vision is a brief, to the point, action-oriented statement that clarifies a core belief about your long-term, positive, parenting goal. Here is a sample vision statement.

To raise our children with love and to help them grow up, learn, and thrive by consistently modeling our positive values every day.

This vision statement is meant as a guide for *all of us*. It is centered on cultivating a loving environment for your children. As such, it provides a positive direction in that the focus is on the process of maturing and developing the skills to grow into a balanced, healthy young adult. The statement also provides a means for how growth happens with regard to aligning your behavior to match your positive values (the concept of positive values is discussed next in Chapter 2). Lastly, the vision statement provides accountability through an expectation as reflected in the reference to everyday actions. It is simple and brief for easy reference and general enough to accommodate diversity through adding your unique style and approach.

One of the assumptions in being a values grounded parent is a commitment and determination to help your children **learn, grow, and thrive**—a universal need for all. This deep-rooted need spans across culture and time—you are wired to grow and develop. Incorporating this in your shared vision helps tap into this powerful **developmental need**. The good news is that your vision provides direction toward a destination—raising your children into healthy, values grounded adults, who then do the same for their children and so on.

So, are you ready to develop your one-of-a-kind shared vision? The following activity will help you and your spouse/partner formulate one. As you craft your vision statement, be sure to include the developmental need for all kids to grow, learn, and thrive.

CHAPTER 1: VISION

ACTIVITY: DEVELOPING YOUR SHARED VISION

Meet with your partner and write out your shared vision statement. If you are a single parent, meet with a trusted adult(s)/family member and do the same.

Some basics in developing a vision:

- Keep it brief—no more than a couple of sentences (get right to the point so you can easily recall and use your vision to guide you, especially when you are dealing with stressful circumstances).

- Keep it simple with proactive and positive words (what will you be doing versus what not to do).

- What is the end result you are hoping for? Make sure your vision statement addresses the future goal.

- Make sure that it is aligned with your parenting purpose as identified in the earlier activity.

- Remember it is a shared vision, so discuss with your co-parent and identify common ground that guides your day-to-day actions.

Don't sweat it if it is not perfect. After writing it down, put it to the side for the night and then re-read it the following day.

Tweak and refine it as needed.

Because of its importance, **write out your shared vision and have it printed.** There are some samples for your reference in Appendix A.

Next, have a family meeting and discuss your shared vision with your kids. Explain the positive nature of your parenting vision and how this guides the day-to-day happenings within your home.

Be sure to frame your vision and hang it where you will be able to see and reference it every day.

So, it is good and well that you have a positive shared vision that helps guide and direct your day-to-day decisions and actions as parents. *However, just like a gym membership, your shared vision is only as good as it is used.* The more you use it, the stronger you become as a leader AND the stronger your family becomes.

Your vision not only helps you remain focused on your positive, long-term, parenting goal, but it also helps you engage in forward thinking. Forward thinking is important as it influences decision making. Let's take a look at the concept of Windshield Thinking as it promotes a proactive approach to parenting.

WINDSHIELD THINKING

Although most of us don't regularly think about it, the windshields on our vehicles serve an important function. They provide safe cover from nature's elements, like wind, rain, dust as well as from road debris. Also, they remind us of the importance of looking forward to where we are going. After all, the windshield is the largest of all windows in the vehicle. Although it can be helpful to know what is behind us as well as to the side, it is important to keep the focus on what lies ahead. This allows us to direct our vehicle and the precious passengers in it to their destination.

Think for a minute and imagine if you *only* looked through the rear-view mirror and side windows in your attempt to take

CHAPTER 1: VISION

your kids to school. What would happen? What would this be like for your children?

Let's briefly revisit the Williams family example as it nicely illustrates how windshield thinking is an outcome of a positive shared vision. Mr. and Mrs. Williams felt that their day-to-day family life was defined by their stressful circumstances surrounding Johnny's volcanic behavior. Much of their thinking and behavior was consumed with how to keep their son calm. This led to Johnny becoming more dependent on them to not upset him. Rather than thinking toward a longer-term, more positive goal, their thinking was focused mostly on the short-term circumstance of Johnny not flipping out (side windows). This short-sighted thinking was fueled by past volcanic episodes (rear-view mirror thinking) and fear that a volcanic episode was on the horizon.

In efforts to become unstuck, the parents defined a shared vision—a vision that reinforced thoughts and behavior toward a long-term, positive goal versus a reactive, short-sighted one. This was a game changer. Since their shared vision was to help Johnny grow into a successful young man through the development of character and positive values, the parents shifted to more forward or windshield thinking on how to best shape his character and teach positive values. As a result of their windshield thinking, they changed their behavior to no longer accept the role of keeping Johnny calm. This was taken a step further to reduce screen time to help reinforce more productive activities with friends and his daredevil brother, Adam.

As the parents changed from rear-view mirror to windshield thinking, guess who also changed his thinking? Yep . . . Johnny. He shifted his thinking to rely less on his parents and more on himself to manage his emotions. When getting upset, he learned to think ahead and identified proactive ways to manage his volcanic feelings. For instance, he went to his room when feeling like hot lava was about to spew from his mouth. He used his room as a safe place to calm himself. He learned the names of various other feelings besides being mad or pissed off. He practiced using feeling words like disappointed, fearful, frustrated, and anxious.

His parents supported him and celebrated his emerging efforts toward growing into a young guy of positive character. As Johnny engaged in more windshield or forward thinking, his behavior changed for the positive and his self-confidence began to swell.

As this example illustrates, a shared vision promotes forward thinking about how one should behave in pursuit of a positive, long-term goal. Windshield thinking is a deliberate process. It involves using your long-term, positive, overall goal or shared vision to influence how you handle all situations with your kids. By doing so, your parenting actions are more aligned with the direction or destination you are hoping to guide your children.

Windshield thinking helps keep the focus on your positive purpose as a parent. By doing so, you switch from your ego and emotions to a more objective and positive goal.

Here are some questions that can help shift your thinking:

- ➪ How is what I am about to do and/or doing aligned with our shared vision?
- ➪ How is my behavior helping our child grow and thrive? What is our child learning from my actions?
- ➪ Am I reacting according to my emotion or am I responding according to our shared vision?

Here are some tips to keep your Shared Vision out of your blind spot and promote windshield thinking:

CHAPTER 1: VISION

- ☑ Use sticky notes to remind you of your shared vision—place them in your car, on the bathroom mirror, and other places to keep it visible.
- ☑ Seek accountability from your spouse/partner and/or a close friend by having that person check with you on how well you are following your vision.
- ☑ Have monthly family meetings—discuss your shared vision and seek feedback on how your family is doing in pursuing this vision.
- ☑ Talk with your kids about windshield thinking and the value it has in their lives.
- ☑ Keep a daily log or journal of your efforts at practicing your shared vision.

TWO FOR ONE

When you consistently practice windshield thinking, you experience a two-for-one savings—talk about great value! The first part is you save yourself from being overly tormented by unnecessary stress from being stuck in the overwhelm of your circumstances. Your shared vision helps you see the bigger picture and not only rise above your adverse circumstances, but also guide your children through them. Secondly, the more you practice forward thinking, the more your children will follow along.

As we will see in the chapter on family culture, how we think and act shapes our family culture, which in turn shapes how we think and act. The more your thinking and day-to-day actions are purposeful and positive, the more your children will absorb this.

SUMMARY AND TAKEAWAYS

- Effective, values grounded parenting starts with a clearly defined vision.
- Vision is your long-term, positive goal as parents. It represents the "why" and purpose behind your role as parents.
- Maintaining a united front with your co-parent strengthens leadership at home
- Your shared vision helps align your day-to-day parenting with a bigger, healthier, and more meaningful purpose.
- Your shared vision helps take the ego out of your parenting approach.
- Diversity in parenting styles is very common and positive as long as these styles are aligned with the shared vision.
- Write down your vision, frame it, and post it in your home. This helps keep your shared vision in your "windshield."
- Share your vision with your children. This way they understand the foundation for your decision making.
- Windshield thinking is an intentional thought process where you use your vision to help guide you in making values grounded decisions AND using these thoughts to direct your behavior.
- When consistently engaging in windshield thinking, you are shaping your family culture and your children will follow along.

CHAPTER 2

POSITIVE VALUES: DEFINING WHAT DEFINES YOU

SUMMERTIME TEMPERATURES in Phoenix typically hover around or above 110 degrees (that is not a typo!). Our family likes to escape the sweltering heat and drive up north to the cool pines of Flagstaff. My in-laws have a cozy cabin nestled near miles of forest land. Over the years, we established a family tradition of fort building, relying on fallen branches along with the occasional toppled tree. My son, known for his passion with construction, often assumed the foreman role. Over the years, he helped design some amazing forts.

One weekend, my in-laws graciously gave us the keys to their cabin. Like most of our trips, the weather did not disappoint, the fort was built, and we were enjoying a neighborhood walk on a lazy afternoon. In the distance, we heard sirens. We did not think much of it. Then came more sirens upon more sirens. The Hot Shot forest fire trucks were racing up and down the streets. As we hurried back to the cabin, we saw a large plume of smoke just over the hill.

An officer from the Flagstaff police approached and explained, "*Sir, we are evacuating the neighborhood. The fire is growing rapidly and heading this direction. Please get your things and leave the premises right away.*"

CHAPTER 2: POSITIVE VALUES

While trying to process this surreal moment, I knew a phone call to my father-in-law was in order. I rang him up, briefly explained the situation, and asked what he wanted us to take and protect for him. As you can imagine, it took him a couple of times to process what exactly was happening. He had just a short minute to identify what was most valuable in their home.

So, before I tell you the outcome of this tense and dangerous situation, put yourself in the shoes of my father-in-law. Imagine you have just a couple of minutes to determine what holds the most value in your home? *What item or items would you take and why? How do you feel on the inside having to make this rushed, yet important, choice?*

Okay, so back to our situation with the encroaching fire and the phone call with my father-in-law. As he attempted to process a multitude of things at once, he paused on the phone, muttered a few inaudible words and then asserted, *"Well, take the family photos from the kitchen and bookcase, a framed collage from my medical school days, and a few of Nonna's art works."* My mother-in-law is a talented artist and several of her paintings nicely decorated their home.

After reassuring him we were all safe, we scrambled to gather the items and load them in the truck. As we were about to pull out, the fire abruptly changed direction with the shift of a southern wind. The evacuation was called off, and their cabin along with the others in the neighborhood were now safe. Whew . . . a close call that left us feeling much relief and gratitude.

As this story illustrates, when we encounter stressful life circumstances, we are pressed to pursue and protect that which has the greatest value in our lives. As a values grounded parent, it is your deeply held beliefs about how you should behave and treat one another that protect you and your kids during the "fires" and crises in your lives.

VALUES GROUNDED PARENTING

VALUES AND CORE BELIEFS

Before delving into the values that define you and your family, let's clarify what is meant by a value. A value represents something of importance, worth, merit, and/or esteem. When used within a context of societal customs, values help define the structure and functioning of a community.

Within the context of values grounded parenting, *a value represents an important core belief that influences and shapes your behavior, relationships, and identity*. For example, let's take a look at the value of respect. Respect reflects a deeply held belief that it is important to show regard for the worth of others and treat others with consideration and care. This belief in turn shapes behavior.

For example, let's say a 4-year-old child screams "NO" when she is reminded that it is time to leave the playground. The mother practices the value of respect by responding to her daughter's protest in a calm, **respectful**, and firm way, stating, "*I understand it is hard to leave (validate). Please think about your words and be respectful, which means talking in a nice way. We need to leave now. So, please put your shoes on and walk quietly with me to the car.*"

As this example illustrates, the mother modeled respect through using a calm, focused tone while redirecting her daughter. She validated her daughter's stress of having to leave the playground and did not let the emotion of the situation overshadow the importance of modeling and teaching respect.

Values come in all different types of shapes and sizes. Most values have a positive influence, though some can have a negative impact. For our intent, we will focus on the positive.

CHAPTER 2: POSITIVE VALUES

THE FOUR ANCHOR VALUES

As you take the next step in defining your positive values, I recommend four Anchor Values that all families ought to embody and practice. The four Anchor Values are humility, gratitude, respect, and accountability.

HUMILITY

Humility is like an antibiotic that protects you and your kids from the ill effects of your pride and ego. It strengthens your social, emotional, and spiritual well-being. It can be defined as being modest and lacking in self-importance. It does not involve thinking less of oneself or devaluing oneself, but thinking about oneself, less. It involves taking your job as a values grounded parent seriously, though not taking yourself so seriously.

It helps keep your shared vision in your windshield, so you stay connected to the overall, long-term, positive goal of helping your kids learn, grow, and thrive. Here are some of the benefits of humility:

- ☑ Humility promotes lifelong learning and a growth mindset.
- ☑ Humility helps you receive, accept, and integrate feedback from others.
- ☑ Humility directs your attention toward what is right versus who is right.
- ☑ Humility moves you to a place of compassionate understanding in your relationships.
- ☑ Humility helps you be more patient and less judgmental.
- ☑ Humility promotes bonding and healthy intimacy.
- ☑ Humility supports accountability.

When you practice humility, you understand that mistakes are part of the process in growing up. Humility helps you stay engaged in all aspects of parenting, so you are consistently learning and growing *with* your children. It helps open you and your kids to accept and integrate feedback from one another, including teachers, coaches, and others involved in your kids' lives.

Humility helps you handle distressing emotions while maintaining a respectful attitude. When you feel disappointed, hurt, angry, or frustrated, you can lessen the strength of this emotion and the tendency to personalize it with a humble respectfulness.

When you embrace humility in your parenting approach, you are more understanding and less likely to take their limit-testing behavior personally. **Practicing humility does not soften your authority as parents; rather, it helps you deal with challenging situations with respect and integrity.** The following example illustrates this.

During our kids' junior-high years, I began to wonder if aliens had taken over their lives. The day-to-day changes in their mood and behavior were simply mystifying. On a few occasions, I had considered calling the Men in Black for help! It was challenging for me as I tried to navigate the boundary between respecting their emerging independence and the need to offer direction and guidance. One of the common struggles we endured involved balancing recreation time and homework.

One afternoon, my son and I found ourselves in a power struggle over getting his homework done. He was busy for a couple of hours making a very cool tank out of Legos. As I entered his room, I explained that it was time for him to get busy with his homework. He became upset and told me, in a matter of words, to stop controlling him. As I attempted to explain, he became more upset and walked away.

Now, in the house I grew up in, walking away from a parent was a blatant sign of disrespect, met with a bellowing command to get my

CHAPTER 2: POSITIVE VALUES

butt back over there. So, you can imagine that I felt a surge of emotion, mostly around feeling dismissed.

Rather than shouting to my son to get his butt back over here, I tried to practice humility, and keep the focus on our shared vision (rather than my upset feelings). By doing so, I was able to think about and acknowledge that my son was relatively new at learning how to grow into his own person. Yelling at him would not offer helpful feedback; rather, it would only serve to make the situation worse and alienate us (speaking of the MIB).

After engaging in some windshield thinking, I approached my son and acknowledged that he had done a great job on his Lego tank (this was a productive activity that I had overlooked earlier). We talked about the different features on it. Then, I asked for us to sit and talk for a few minutes. I clarified that I had no interest in controlling him. Rather, I wanted to support him growing into a strong, values grounded young man (shared vision). I explained that part of growing up involves putting aside pleasurable things in order to take care of his responsibilities. We talked about the toughness it takes to do what is right.

He said that he understood and would work on it. He also provided helpful feedback to me. He explained that I can be abrupt and I repeat myself too much. I told him that I understood and I would work on it.

Lastly, I explained that when he walks away from me when I am talking to him, it comes across as dismissive and disrespectful. He clarified that it was not his intention. Rather, he wanted to walk away because he was upset and needed to chill. We both agreed it was a positive response AND he needs to say something to that effect before he walks away to avoid any misunderstanding. We hugged, and he got busy with his homework.

As this example illustrates, practicing humility enabled us to sit and talk about a conflict that ultimately helped both of us grow. As the parent, I took the lead and tried to be humble in my approach. Instead of yelling or engaging in a power struggle, we both expressed ourselves respectfully and used the situation as a meaningful learning opportunity. By trying to be humble, we experienced that our shared vision is not merely words but *words to live by*. My son and I grew in our positive intimacy and trust as a result.

HUMILITY & VULNERABILITY

Consistently practicing humility is tough because it often leads to a place of vulnerability. You may find yourself feeling vulnerable as you encounter situations where you don't quite know what the heck to do. For example, your kids may ask innocently on the way to the grocery store, "Where do babies come from?" Or, they may ask, "Why do you yell at me if it is not okay to yell?" These questions, and many others like them, help invite meaningful consideration and conversation. When your children speak up this way, it is good to model humility in your response.

When you find yourself in parenting situations where you are vulnerable and uncertain, turn to your shared vision for guidance. Ask yourself, "What is my positive purpose as a parent?" Although you probably will not identify the perfect response, seeking your vision will help you uncover different options for handling unforeseen issues.

Although I have been a clinical psychologist for over 25 years and a parent for 20 years, I find myself being humbled by how much there is to learn. When I am stumped and uncertain how to handle or talk about a situation, I often say something like:

CHAPTER 2: POSITIVE VALUES

"I am not certain how best to talk about this. However, I know it is important for us to do so. So, let's give it a try and see what happens. If we make mistakes, that's okay. It is better to try than avoid it altogether."

Humility helps cultivate an attitude to better manage difficult and stressful situations without compromising one's positive values. Undoubtedly, this is a tough balance, though being tough and balanced is a central part in being a values grounded parent.

Here are some practical tips and suggestions on practicing humility:

- ☑ Remind yourself daily of your shared vision, keeping your focus on the long-term, positive goal in raising your children.
    - ✓ Write your vision down on sticky notes and place them in your car and bathroom.
    - ✓ Put your shared vision statement as a screen saver on your phone.
- ☑ Admit when you are wrong, apologize, and seek forgiveness.
- ☑ Ask for help and seek support from others.
    - ✓ Remind yourself that parenting is a humbling, on-the-job learning experience.
- ☑ Listen twice as much as you talk—there is a reason why our good Lord gave us two ears and one mouth.
- ☑ Seek feedback from your spouse/partner and children. For example, ask, "How am I doing as a parent? What areas can I improve?"
    - ✓ Identify one area in which you can improve as a parent and ask your family to hold you accountable.

GRATITUDE

Gratitude is like the "warm blanket on a cold day" value. It feels good to receive *and* to give it. It promotes an attitude of appreciation and thankfulness. Gratitude is the heart of the four Anchor Values, and humility is the soul. By practicing gratitude, you feel valued and appreciated as well as give value to others.

Grateful parents raise grateful kids. By demonstrating and encouraging gratitude in your children, you are setting a foundation for longstanding happiness. A key developmental task for your children is to find ways to experience genuine joy and happiness. Teaching and encouraging gratitude opens the door for such discovery to take place.

Happier and healthier children are far more responsive to your values grounded parenting efforts. On the other hand, ungrateful children are far more difficult to parent, often focusing on what they don't have rather than being grateful for what they do. This mindset causes protests and power struggles fueled by an entitled attitude of "what's in this for me?"

Veruca Salt, one of the characters in the movie *Willy Wonka and the Chocolate Factory*, is a terrific example of an ungrateful child. She has an insatiable appetite for material things and getting her way ALL the time. This is fostered from indulgent parents with few, if any, healthy boundaries. The more her parents feed her entitlement, the emptier and lonelier she becomes. One can clearly see this is a child who is in deep need of values grounded parents.

TEACHING GRATITUDE

Teaching and practicing gratitude occurs in different ways. Some are quick and easy, and others involve more time. A quick and easy way is to generate a list of three things to be grateful for—every day. In our home, we have discussed this over a family meal. Sometimes this occurs through a conversation and other times through prayer. This helps expand our awareness of gratitude not only as individuals, but as a family. Another quick and easy way is to leave a reminder note for your kids

CHAPTER 2: POSITIVE VALUES

before they leave for school. For example, I would put sticky notes at my kids' place settings with the question, "What are you grateful for today?"

Some other ways to teach gratitude involve serving others who are less fortunate. One year, my daughter and I made brown bag lunches for the homeless. As she handed them out, she received various responses. Some grateful, some paranoid, and some silent with a look of wonder. The conversation on the way home was quite meaningful as we processed what it would be like to live on the streets and how grateful we are to have a safe home. Rather than obsessing about getting the latest, greatest electronic device, my daughter was feeling grateful for having food in the pantry and easy access to flush toilets.

We also served at our local food shelter. As my son was serving dinner, I will never forget the look on his face when a homeless boy, about his age, held up his plate for some mac 'n' cheese. I could talk gratitude till I was blue in the face and it would come nowhere near what my son experienced in that moment. The conversation we had on the way home was quite meaningful. We pondered questions like: Where does the young boy sleep? How did he become homeless? How does a family become homeless? We enjoyed our dinner that night with a humble appreciation for the blessing of a home and warm meal.

Another way to support gratitude is to set boundaries and limits on ungrateful behavior. By redirecting ungrateful behavior, you help your children see the emptiness underlying their actions. When this happens, you can lead and guide them to more grateful ways of thinking and behaving. The following example illustrates this.

The Jacksons, a family of four, were having mounting difficulties with Angela, their oldest daughter. Angela was going into her third year in high school. Maria, Angela's younger sister, was in junior high.

Her parents explained that as long as Angela got her way, things were fine. When they said "No" to anything she wanted, the fireworks

VALUES GROUNDED PARENTING

started. She would yell, calling them horrible parents and blaming them for making her life miserable. She would become quite emotional, telling them tearfully, "You make me depressed!" The parents felt blamed and guilty and then would give in to what Angela wanted. Worse yet, Maria started to follow in her sister's footprints.

On the outside, Angela got what she wanted, accumulating lots of stuff. On the inside, however, her self-esteem was eroding, becoming more and more empty. As Angela devalued her parents and friends, her own sense of value and worth was crumbling.

The parents had stylistic differences in their parenting approach. The father was overly strict and the mother tended to be lenient. Angela reacted to her father's strict approach with willful defiance. When her mother attempted to set limits, Angela reacted with dismissiveness. Bottom line was that Angela got her way. The parents were not only becoming increasingly frustrated with her, but also with each other.

The parents agreed that they struggled with maintaining a *United Front*. With that said, they pledged to work on being more unified and agreed that clear boundaries, limits, and discipline needed to be set and enforced.

The weekend was fast approaching, and Angela *told* her parents that she was going to the Friday night game and then hanging out at a friend's house all weekend. She demanded some money for dinner and the movies. She also informed her parents that her new phone was missing and she needed a replacement. The parents knew that they needed to set limits on her growing entitlement.

As a step toward maintaining a United Front, the parents developed a shared vision: *To raise our daughters with solid values so they will grow into healthy young women.* Next, they shared it with both daughters. The parents discussed gratitude at one of their family meetings along with other important values. The children participated as well

CHAPTER 2: POSITIVE VALUES

and identified a set of positive values. Interestingly, Angela agreed with her parents that gratitude should be one of their family's values. They explained that boundaries, limits, and consequences would be consistently used to support their growth into positive young women.

The parents remained steadfast in their efforts at supporting one another in setting and reinforcing limits with Angela. The emotional fireworks continued for a few weeks, though the intensity was decreasing. Both parents worked at becoming more balanced in their approach to limit setting as well as backing the other up. They also rewarded behavior that reflected gratitude and respect. Things like use of the car, gas card, and phone were contingent upon Angela behaving respectfully, responsibly, and gratefully.

Angela learned the value of earning privileges versus demanding them. As her behavior changed, so did her mood and self-esteem. Angela acknowledged feeling better about herself, describing various improvements in her ability at handling stressful situations at home and school.

As often is the case, Maria followed in her sister's shoes, showing greater cooperation and respect. Both sisters appreciated their emerging maturity and encouraged each other to keep feeding it with gratitude and other important family values.

As the above examples illustrate, the practice of gratitude opens the minds and hearts of children to look beyond themselves and see a bigger, healthier picture. Whether it involves serving those less fortunate or being held accountable for respectful and grateful behavior, you are teaching them to think more positively about themselves, others, and their life. One of the positive consequences in teaching gratitude is the emergence of appreciation and genuine happiness. In its purest form, gratitude is not only experienced within the positives of life, but also the challenges.

VALUES GROUNDED PARENTING

Here are some practical tips for growing gratitude:

- ☑ Ask your children to research the positive effects of gratitude on physical and emotional health—for younger children, do the research together.
    - ✓ Ask your kids to share their findings during a family meeting.
    - ✓ Ask one another to identify a difficult life situation you endured, and what you learned to be grateful for as a result.
- ☑ During family mealtime, ask three things for which each family member is grateful.
- ☑ While tucking your children in bed, talk about what you are grateful for and ask the same from them.
- ☑ During holidays like Martin Luther King, Jr. Day and Memorial Day, talk with your kids about gratitude for the selfless acts of others.
    - ✓ Ask your kids to write a thank-you note for our veterans and active military personnel.
    - ✓ Consider https://www.operationgratitude.com/express-your-thanks/write-letters/.
- ☑ Have a movie night and rent *Willy Wonka and the Chocolate Factory* (I recommend the original version). Talk as a family about the difference between Charlie and Veruca Salt in terms of gratitude. Who seemed to be happier and why?
- ☑ Adopt a charity and serve as a family.

Practicing gratitude helps protect your family from selfishness and leads you toward selflessness. In fact, when you practice gratitude consistently, you become more humble. Gratitude and humility are fertilizers for positive relationships and intimacy.

CHAPTER 2: POSITIVE VALUES

RESPECT

A good example of respect is reflected in the Golden Rule—treat others as you wish to be treated. When you are respectful with each other, you are more likely to feel cared for and valued. It helps you grow trust and positive intimacy.

When you don't practice respect, your relationships falter. "Hurt people, *hurt* people." This saying describes one of the less attractive qualities within humans. When someone hurts you, it is common to want to hurt them or others in return. This negative cycle can wreak havoc in your families.

Respect, however, can help you break the cycle. It invites you to take the high road, raising the bar for how you manage your own hurt, pain, anger, and frustration. When you engage respect, you shift from being reactive to being responsive.

As a psychologist, I developed a specialty in working with children who have anger management problems. These are the kids who act on impulse, cursing a teacher and/or parent, punching holes in walls, getting in fights and brawls with others, and exhibiting stubborn defiance. When describing the problem that brought them to therapy, many of the kids state that anger is the problem. If they weren't so angry, they would not be in trouble or have problems. Their misguided solution is simply not to get angry.

The feeling of anger is not what gets them in trouble. The problem is how they choose to manage it AND express it. To illustrate this point, I tell them the following story:

I once knew a teenager who was charged with aggravated assault. He became enraged at a classmate because he stole money from him. He beat this kid up so bad that he was hospitalized for a couple of days. When the judge read the charges, he did not say, "You are being charged with feeling enraged" or "You are being charged with feeling incredibly angry."

VALUES GROUNDED PARENTING

Rather, he was being charged with how he managed (or mismanaged) and expressed his anger.

This unfortunate story illustrates the value of expressing difficult and highly stressful emotions in respectful and safe ways. Although many kids think that avoiding the feeling of anger is the way to go, they actually become less and less skilled at learning how to manage and express it. The less skillful they are, the less confident they become. The less confident they are in themselves, the more they rely on others to manage their feelings for them. This can be a dangerous cycle.

One way to break this self-defeating cycle is to lean into the discomfort of the emotion and practice healthy ways of expression. I discuss with parents and children the value of learning and practicing how to express one's emotions respectfully. Oftentimes, kids comment, "I have no control over my anger" or "It is too hard" to express anger in respectful ways. This is where the shared vision of growing up in a healthy way plays a key role. In order for one to grow up and thrive, one must learn how to express anger and other stressful feelings respectfully.

When you consistently practice respect, you not only manage the highs and lows of parenthood, but you model for your children how to manage the highs and lows of growing up. You show them how to take the high road and use respect to protect the integrity of their relationships.

The activity on the following page will help clarify what respect looks like.

CHAPTER 2: POSITIVE VALUES

ACTIVITY: DEFINING AND SHOWING RESPECT

Gather your family for a meeting. Explain that you would like to learn and talk more about respect, especially as it is practiced within your family.

Play Aretha Franklin's "Respect" song for everyone. You can quickly find a version on YouTube or download the song on another app.

Discuss the following:

- How would you define respect?
- How do you show respect?
    - What words can you say to show respect?
    - What actions can you do that will show respect?
- Why is respect important for our family?
- Do you feel respected in our family?

Talk with your family about the importance of expressing stressful feelings like anger, hurt, disappointment, fear, and frustration in respectful ways.

Here are some tips and suggestions for practicing respect:

- ☑ Use positive and encouraging words.
- ☑ Try to listen TWICE as much as you talk—if you want

your kids to listen to you, lead the way by first listening to them.
- ☑ Close to 90 percent of communication is nonverbal (posture, facial expression) and para-verbal (tone, volume). Be mindful of how your nonverbal and para-verbal behavior demonstrate respect.
- ☑ Set up reminders around the house regarding the Golden Rule—treat others as you wish to be treated.
- ☑ Consistently practice expressing emotions in a direct, calm, and respectful manner that supports the dignity of other family members.
- ☑ Avoid using sarcasm in emotional situations; it leads to family members feeling dismissed, devalued, and disrespected.
- ☑ When emotionally triggered and upset, take time to cool down, to allow the emotion to settle before speaking or addressing others.
- ☑ Practice respect when texting one another and using devices to communicate.

Although I counsel kids and families on respectful ways of handling anger and other snarky feelings, please know that as a parent I struggle just like the rest of us. There are times when I get frustrated and blurt out something hurtful to my kids. These times offer reminders of re-engaging the value of humility, which in turn helps lead to being more respectful. Over time, I have found that practicing respect becomes habit forming with fewer blurt-outs and less of a need to have a "back-space button" to erase a hurtful action.

ACCOUNTABILITY

Accountability is the "ownership value" as it promotes personal responsibility for one's behavior. It connects the ideal behind a value to specific

CHAPTER 2: POSITIVE VALUES

actions that demonstrate or perform this ideal. When you practice accountability, you become like a chef or a baker and your values are like recipes. You take the recipe, roll up your sleeves, and get busy making the dish. Like most chefs, there is a learning curve to transforming an idea into a creation. However, in order to learn, you simply gotta get in the kitchen and try. Accountability involves taking your values and aligning your behavior to match them.

As an example, let's revisit the Jackson family, whose daughter Angela behaved in ungrateful and entitled ways. She blamed her parents for her emotional outbursts and disrespectful behavior. Supporting positive change for Angela needed to start with accountability. If the parents expected Angela to change her ways, the first step was for them to accept accountability in setting clear and consistent limits on their daughter's negative behavior. The limits and consequences served to alert Angela that her behavior was problematic and ungrounded in the values of respect, accountability, and gratitude. The more ownership or accountability the parents assumed, the greater the consistency they demonstrated. The more consistent they were, the greater the kids trusted that their parents would reinforce the boundaries and consequences.

For example, Angela learned that it was a privilege and not her right to have use of her parents' car. The parents took accountability or ownership in setting up and enforcing behavior expectations necessary for Angela to earn the privilege of using the family car. Such behavior expectations were identified in a proactive manner and included using respectful language, completing chores, showing gratitude and appreciation for privileges, and maintaining at least a B average in school. Part of the parents' accountability meant obtaining regular updates from her school and checking to make sure Angela's daily and weekend chores were completed.

Angela had a history of making empty promises in changing her negative behavior as a way to get her parents to lift consequences. The parents accepted accountability to stand their ground and not be swayed by short-lived promises. The parents pledged to keep a United Front and to back each other up with the discipline and consequences.

As anticipated, the more accountability the parents demonstrated, the more ownership Angela accepted for making positive changes to her behavior. In her efforts to change, Angela certainly made mistakes. When she messed up and said hurtful and ungrateful things, she sought to make amends by apologizing (this helped her learn more about humility).

Angela learned to accept accountability for expressing her strong feelings in respectful ways. For instance, rather than yelling at her parents, she learned to practice communicating her feelings directly without shouting, cursing, or threatening. She also learned to walk away, do some deep breathing, and go to her room to chill out. These changes in Angela moved her out of her comfort zone where she was growing in a new direction.

The parents were also prone to yelling and saying hurtful things when upset with their daughter. They too practiced humility by apologizing, making amends, and restoring positive intimacy in their relationship with their daughter. In order to set the example for her to follow, they practiced expressing their frustration and anger in respectful ways. For instance, they reminded each other to use a calm tone, use behavioral versus emotional words when redirecting Angela's behavior (saying things like "please use a calm tone and respectful words when talking to me" versus "you're rude and nasty!"). As the parents accepted greater ownership for expressing their strong feelings, they set a great values grounded example for Angela.

As Angela practiced greater accountability for behaving in accord with values like respect and humility, she earned greater trust with her parents, not to mention privileges. She began to walk with a swagger of confidence, feeling more control over her behavior. Showing gratitude at home and with friends became more natural for her. In her words, "My parents nor do I put up with my B.S. anymore . . . I don't want to be *that* ungrateful kid. I feel more mature and confident." Maria, Angela's younger sister, was happy to see such positive values being practiced a lot more consistently at home. As anticipated, she followed in her older sister's footsteps.

These changes took some time, practice, and patience on everyone's part. Additionally, the family understood that being values grounded is a lifelong pursuit, not just for times of trouble or difficulty. They needed to stay grounded and accountable for behaving in accord with their values; otherwise, they would go back to their drama.

The Jackson family example nicely illustrates that without accountability, values remain only as ideals. You miss wonderful opportunities to learn how to practice them and see how they help your family grow and thrive as a result. The more you practice accountability, the greater your self-confidence grows at being values grounded.

FAST FOOD VERSUS HOME COOKING

We live in fast food culture where most of us want things right away with little to no waiting. We become easily impatient if we have to wait, whether it be for an app on our phone to work or if we are in line at the local coffee shop getting coffee.

SPOILER ALERT: Practicing your values takes time, persistence, and patience. You run the risk of watering down accountability if you rush and take shortcuts.

Practicing accountability as a values grounded parent is analogous to home cooking. It takes time, yet the process and outcome are hearty and quite healthy. It is **hearty** on two levels: first, it shows love; second, it is fulfilling. Accountability ensures that you are earnest in your efforts

VALUES GROUNDED PARENTING

at following your recipe comprised of a shared vision, the four Anchor Values, and a constellation of other positive values. If you try to rush raising your kids and growing your values, you will likely end up with a microwave meal—lacking important nutrients. Values grounded parenting is much more like a Crock-Pot recipe.

Here are some tips and suggestions for practicing accountability:

- ☑ Write down your house rules/behavior expectations and post them so everyone sees them and holds each other accountable.
- ☑ Be consistent with boundaries, limits, and discipline.
- ☑ Maintain a United Front with your spouse/partner—back them up in their efforts at reinforcing the rules.
- ☑ Take the lead at demonstrating the values of respect, gratitude, humility, and accountability.
- ☑ Use an organizer and daily to-do lists to increase follow-through.
- ☑ When asking your children to do various tasks, take the time to follow up with them to ensure accountability.
- ☑ Keep an accountability jar at home.
  - ✓ Every time you catch your kids being accountable, put a marble in it. Once the jar is filled, you do a fun family activity together.
  - ✓ Even if your children goof up and make a mistake, if they are accountable, they still earn a marble.
- ☑ Do monthly one-on-one activities with your kids, for example, taking a neighborhood walk, having breakfast, hiking, playing a board game, and so on. During your one-on-one time, ask for your child's feedback on how you are doing as a parent (this feedback is an accountability check on how well you are practicing and modeling the values for your kids).

CHAPTER 2: POSITIVE VALUES

- ☑ Admit your mistakes, acknowledge the impact your behavior has on your kids, and make amends. Take the lead in showing your kids how to step up and be accountable.
- ☑ When your kids make mistakes, hold them accountable.
  - ✓ Avoid yelling, blaming, and shaming them. Shaming reduces accountability and increases avoidance.
  - ✓ Stay calm, and use consequences to help them learn from their mistakes.
- ☑ Discuss your positive values during family meals.

Accountability means you step up and make earnest efforts at being values grounded, though by no means being a perfect parent. So, when you goof up, it is important to accept accountability for your behavior, admit your mistake(s), and make amends. By doing so, you strengthen your role as a leader in your family. Your kids will trust you more and will feel safe to acknowledge their mistakes as well. When you can discuss mistakes and lessons learned, you grow positive intimacy and closeness as a family.

ADDING VALUE

The next step after establishing the four Anchor Values is to identify and define other values that support your shared vision. In addition to the four Anchors, I recommend five to seven more. As a reminder, *a value represents a core belief that shapes your behavior, relationships, and identity.* Below are some questions for you and your kids to discuss:

- ⇨ What do you find valuable about your family?
- ⇨ What values should you practice as a family?
- ⇨ What is valuable about your relationships with each other?
- ⇨ Identify three values that will help you grow up. Explain how these values help you grow.

VALUES GROUNDED PARENTING

Sometimes labeling a value can be difficult. Below is a list of some values that may fit for you and your family:

Perseverance/Persistence	Honesty	Generosity
Discipline	Integrity	Hard work
Responsibility	Kindness	Fairness
Dependability	Commitment	Openness
Dignity/Honor	Family	Faith
Courage/Valor	Moderation	Peace
Transparency	Diversity	Self-control/Restraint
Creativity/Innovation	Diligence	Stewardship
Love	Sincerity	Thoughtfulness
Playfulness/Humor	Devotion	Curiosity
Altruism	Awareness	Trustworthiness
Productivity Being constructive	Loyalty	Positivity
Teamwork	Toughness	Affection
Compassion	Dedication	Consistency

DEFINING MOMENTS

Now that you have defined the values that define you, the next step is to define the behavior that demonstrates these values. As discussed in the section on accountability, this is the recipe that makes the value. ***It is key to define your values with a specific behavior or behaviors.*** Otherwise, the value remains a noble sounding concept with no real-world application.

Here are some tips and strategies for defining your values:

- ☑ Identify what you would say or do that shows you are practicing this value.
- ☑ Identify a behavior for how you can practice this value at home, school, work, and with friends.
- ☑ Write down these behaviors next to each value. (The process of documenting it makes it more real and increases accountability.)

Be sure to write your values down and post them in a visible place(s) in your home. The more visible your values are, the more you are reminded of their importance.

SUMMARY AND TAKEAWAYS

- A value represents an important core belief that influences and shapes your behavior, relationships, and identity.
- Teaching and developing values is much like home cooking versus microwave meals. It requires a purposeful and deliberate effort with continued practice.
- Humility, gratitude, respect, and accountability are the four Anchor Values that all families ought to include in their efforts to accomplish their shared vision.
- Humility helps take the ego out of parenting, promoting healthy ways of managing stress, dealing with mistakes, and seeking support.

- Gratitude leads to longstanding happiness, a positive perspective, and protects you and your family from the ill effects of entitlement.
- Respect protects your relationships from the ill effects of reactive anger and destructive conflict. It represents the Golden Rule.
- Accountability bridges the ideal of a value to real-world practice. It is the effort and practice of making the value real within yourself and your relationships.
- As with all values, the four Anchor Values take time to develop and help grow trust, positive intimacy, and family closeness.
- Values need to be behaviorally defined so you and your kids know how to demonstrate and practice them.

CHAPTER 3

FAMILY CULTURE AND YOUR FAMILY BLUEPRINT

AS A THIRD-YEAR doctoral student, I moved to China Town in Oakland, California. It was a wonderful experience being immersed within the culture. I learned much about the families and community. When walking through the neighborhood, I could see the culture come alive through various community celebrations, delicious food, large family gatherings at the park, beautiful artwork, or Sunday service. It is one thing to read about culture, though it is much more meaningful to experience and live within it.

CULTURE IN A BROAD SENSE

Culture relates to the customs and beliefs that shape and define groups of people. It influences our society, government, communities, neighborhoods, schools, businesses, and families. We experience it in movies, art, music, media, food, department stores, and language. It shapes our beliefs and attitudes about many things like success, happiness, masculinity, femininity, intimacy, and our sense of purpose. We are all influenced by culture, whether we are conscious of it or not.

CHAPTER 3: FAMILY CULTURE AND YOUR FAMILY BLUEPRINT

As values grounded parents, it is important to be conscious of the meaningful impact culture has on you and your family. It is through this awareness that you can develop and define your own, one-of-a-kind, family culture. Since many of your current beliefs and attitudes about parenting and family functioning come from what you learned growing up, let's explore the value of your family blueprint.

THE FAMILY BLUEPRINT

Blueprints are developed by architects and used to help convert a design idea into a real-life, working structure. As the executive director of a private day school, I had the opportunity to work with an architect named Andy. Through his work, I saw firsthand how a series of blueprints helped expand and transform the space within our campus, ultimately benefitting the day-to-day programming for our students.

As a values grounded parent, you are like an architect. You have ideas for how your family ought to be constructed. The wonderful challenge is translating these blueprint ideas into a day-to-day, real-world, healthy, functioning family.

During our work together on improving the school, Andy often provided recommendations on how we should proceed with the design. These recommendations, he'd say, were based on prior experience and lessons learned from other projects. It was apparent that our school blueprint was informed by many other blueprints that came before us.

Similarly, your current family blueprint is significantly influenced by the blueprints that came before you. Examining the family design with which you were raised is an important task as this often informs your current family blueprint. Like most blueprints, it is a framework, though the structure often changes to meet new life demands and circumstances.

These blueprints inform you how to be as parents *and* how not to be. Learning and growth happens in both areas. As I have explained to others who have grown up with dysfunction in their families (which is most of us), the goal is to dilute and limit the dysfunction and amplify the positive, healthy, and functional aspects of your original family design.

As a family architect, you have a rare and wonderful opportunity to create a blueprint that will shape your family culture. You have the opportunity to preserve important family traditions and perhaps create new ones. This is meaningful and rewarding work. There are two parts to this work. The first step is to examine and review the blueprint from which you were raised. The second step is to develop and refine your current blueprint, aligning it with your shared vision and positive values.

The following two activities will help you with this. Take your time with both parts of these activities. Your family blueprint is an important part of your foundation in pursuing your shared vision.

ACTIVITY I: MY FAMILY OF ORIGIN BLUEPRINT

Below are important family design topics for you and your partner to review and discuss. If you are a single parent, discuss these topics with a trusted adult / family member. Be sure to be respectful and humble as you discuss these important blueprint areas.

In your reflections and discussions, keep in mind a "both/and" perspective as opposed to an "either/or" view. That is, most of us have had BOTH positive AND negative experiences as opposed to EITHER positive OR negative experiences. So, as you reflect, I encourage you to address both the positive and negative. Please know that exploration of these topics is quite valuable as it offers an opportunity to clarify and shape your family culture.

EXPECTATIONS:

- What were the expectations in your home growing up?
- How were these expectations defined and discussed?
- Were there certain areas, like school or work, that were more clearly defined?
- Did your parents walk the talk? That is, did they follow and model the expectations they had of you and your siblings?
- Which expectations were helpful? Why? Which expectations were not helpful? Why?
- How does your experience of these expectations in your family of origin influence the expectations you have in your current family?

VALUES GROUNDED PARENTING

RULES:
- What were the rules in your family growing up?
- Were rules clearly defined?
- Were rules consistently enforced? Did one parent assume the role of disciplinarian?
- What parts of your family rules were helpful/unhelpful?
- How does your experience of these rules in your family of origin influence the rules you have in your current family?

COMMUNICATION:
- Describe how you communicated as a family. Did communication tend to be direct or indirect?
- Did you have family meetings?
- What was your communication around family values?
- What parts of family communication were helpful/unhelpful?
- How does this experience of communication in your family of origin influence how you communicate in your current family?

BOUNDARIES:
- How were boundaries defined in your family growing up?
- Were the roles of a parent and those of a child clearly defined AND followed?
- Were your parents in charge and provide clear expectations?
- What aspects of boundaries were helpful/unhelpful?
- How do your experiences of boundaries in your family of origin influence how you define and apply boundaries with your children?

EMOTION:
- How was emotion expressed in your family growing up?
- What kind of emotional vocabulary did your parents have?
- What were the more common emotions experienced in your family?
- How does this experience of emotion in your family of origin influence how you manage and express feelings in your current family?

LOVE/INTIMACY:
- Describe the love and intimacy in your family.
- How was affection expressed?
- Describe how love was communicated in your family.
- What aspects of this intimacy did you find helpful/unhelpful?
- How does this experience of intimacy in your family of origin influence how you express love and intimacy in your current family?

STRUCTURE:
- Describe the day-to-day structure or routine in your family growing up.
- Was there a clearly defined structure on weekdays and weekends?

- What parts of the structure/routine were helpful/unhelpful?
- How does your experience of structure and routine in your family of origin influence how you approach structure and routine with your current family?

LEADERSHIP:

- Who was the leader or leaders in your family growing up?
- How would you describe their leadership style?
- What parts of their leadership were helpful/unhelpful?
- How does your experience of the leadership impact how you and your spouse/co-parent seek to be leaders in your family?

DECISION MAKING:

- How were decisions made in your family growing up?
- Were certain decisions considered "executive decisions" made only by your parents? If so, describe. How were these decisions different from others?
- What parts of the decision-making process were helpful/unhelpful?
- How does your experience of decision making in your family of origin influence how you make decisions with your current family?

CHAPTER 3: FAMILY CULTURE AND YOUR FAMILY BLUEPRINT

> **DISCIPLINE:**
> - How was discipline handled in your family growing up?
> - Was one parent more of a disciplinarian than the other? Was the discipline consistent? What parts of discipline did you find helpful/unhelpful?
> - How does your experience of discipline in your family of origin influence how you handle discipline with your current family?

Now that you have reviewed and reflected on your family-of-origin blueprint, the next step is to develop and create your current blueprint. The following activity will help guide you in this effort.

VALUES GROUNDED PARENTING

ACTIVITY II: DEVELOPING YOUR CURRENT FAMILY BLUEPRINT AND DESIGN

In this activity, get together with your spouse/co-parent to review, discuss and document your design and plans for your family. If you are a sole parent, get together with a family member or family friend to discuss. Be sure to practice humility and respect (part of the 4 Anchors) in how you talk and listen to one another, avoiding judgment and sarcasm.

- Expectations
- Rules
- Emotion
- Intimacy
- Structure/Routine
- Communication
- Leadership
- Decision making
- Discipline

As you discuss each area, identify how it aligns with your shared vision (parenting purpose) and positive values. Write it down as this makes your family design a living document. Below are a couple of samples.

CHAPTER 3: FAMILY CULTURE AND YOUR FAMILY BLUEPRINT

- ✎ **FOUNDATIONAL AREA:** Discipline
- ✎ **SHARED VISION (PARENTING PURPOSE):** Our purpose in using discipline is to support our children practicing self-discipline, respect, accountability, self-control, and humility, which is aligned with our shared vision of (state your shared vision here).
- ✎ **VALUES:** By disciplining our children, we are supporting and growing the values of accountability, respect, humility, self-control, integrity, and self-discipline.
- ✎ **PUTTING DISCIPLINE INTO PRACTICE:** We pledge to have a united front in backing each other up with disciplining our kids. We will focus discipline on supporting values grounded behavior as opposed to making it personal. When we disagree about discipline, we will respectfully resolve the issue away from the children. We will positively reinforce our children when they show self-discipline. We will consistently and respectfully use boundaries, limits, and consequences when they make mistakes.
- ✎ **FOUNDATIONAL AREA:** Emotion
- ✎ **SHARED VISION (PARENTING PURPOSE):** Understanding, managing, and expressing emotion in healthy ways is key to having healthy, intimate, and balanced relationships, which supports our shared vision of (state your shared vision here).

- **VALUES:** By encouraging and supporting healthy emotional expression, we are supporting and growing the values of love, compassion, trust, respect, togetherness, and empathy.
- **PUTTING EMOTIONAL COMMUNICATION INTO PRACTICE:** We pledge to be mindful and encouraging of healthy emotional expression. We understand that feelings are neither right nor wrong, and we will work as a family to understand and validate each other's emotions even when we disagree as to why one feels the way they do. When we are stressed and upset, we will encourage and support respectful ways of expressing these strong feelings. We will consistently use positive and negative consequences, boundaries, and limits as a means to encourage and support positive and healthy emotional expression.

In the above samples, the foundational area is aligned with the shared vision and positive values. The sense of purpose is clear as is the values it supports.

If there are other foundational areas that are not on the list that you deem important, include those. Once completed, your family design will serve as a useful reference.

Be sure to share your blueprint with your children, perhaps during a family meeting.

CHAPTER 3: FAMILY CULTURE AND YOUR FAMILY BLUEPRINT

STRUCTURED FLEXIBILITY

Andy the architect also pointed out that unforeseen issues often surface when the construction crew attempts to follow the blueprint. When redesigning our school, the crew had to move a few walls, redirect a water pipe, and reconfigure some electrical lines to ensure that proper codes were followed. Undoubtedly, we had to be flexible while still maintaining the integrity of the design.

Your family blueprint is no different. Unforeseen issues and unique life circumstances often surface. They require you to adapt and be flexible while still following your shared vision and positive values. Maintaining ***structured flexibility*** will help you navigate and adapt without compromising your values and vision. Structured flexibility involves keeping your structure while adapting to unforeseen life circumstances.

CULTURE BOARD

After developing your family blueprint, the next step is the family culture board. This board serves to highlight your positive values, shared vision, and aspects of your family design. Culture building occurs when three things happen: 1) Clearly defining the values and beliefs that represent your culture; 2) Consistent practice of these highly regarded values; 3) Mindful and intentional efforts to make your values and shared vision ***visible***.

Your culture board keeps your positive values and parenting purpose visible. The following activity provides the steps in constructing your family culture board. A sample culture board can be found on the Values Grounded Parenting website (www.valuesgrounded.com under the "parenting" heading).

ACTIVITY II: CONSTRUCTING YOUR ONE-OF-A-KIND FAMILY CULTURE BOARD

STEP 1:
Purchase a couple of large poster boards and some cool and fun art supplies. Let your creativity flow with this—consider using supplies like scented markers, stickers, crayons, photos, colored pencils, and so on. This makes the activity much more enjoyable and meaningful, and it invites participation from your kids.

STEP 2:
Gather your family and set aside 1½ to 2 hours to work on your board. Find a place where you can all work on the board together.

When introducing your Culture Board to your kids, start with the purpose, explaining and discussing what culture is (refer to the beginning of this chapter for a brief explanation) and the value in clarifying your family culture. Have your list of positive values on hand for easy reference and be sure to highlight the importance of documenting these values, positive attributes of your family, and your shared vision.

Encourage laughter, out-of-the-box thinking, and reflection. Make it a fun experience—it doesn't hurt to play some cool tunes (music list that everyone gets to choose) and munch on some popcorn or other tasty treats.

CHAPTER 3: FAMILY CULTURE AND YOUR FAMILY BLUEPRINT

STEP 3:
I recommend that each family member uses a pencil first before using a permanent marker, crayon, etc. Although mistake making is part of any family culture, using a pencil helps limit too many mistakes and allows for family members to try a few designs before they make one permanent.

STEP 4:
Be sure to title your one-of-a-kind family culture board by writing your last name in relatively large letters. On our board, I wrote in big block letters, "Redivo Family Culture" smack dab in the center. All the positive values and family design practices encircle our name—sort of like insulating and protecting us.

STEP 5:
Let your creative juices flow as you capture your values that define your culture. There are many ways to design your board: you can write down the values, cut the words out from a magazine and glue them, put in photos of your family (extended family as well), use symbols or pictures that describe positive values you aspire to as a family. For example, in our family culture board, I took a piece of duct tape and stuck it on the board. On the duct tape, using a Sharpie marker, I wrote the words, "Toughness" and "Work Ethic." My wife identified a positive value for each letter of our last name and wrote them in. My son wrote "POSITIVITY" and put a smiling sun for the 'O'. My daughter drew a happy face and wrote the word "Laughter" over the smile.

STEP 6:
Once completed, be sure to have all family members sign the board, making it like a Declaration.

STEP 7:
Get your family culture board framed. This will be an added cost, yet take a moment to think... How valuable is being reminded of your values and culture? How important is it for you as a family to make your foundation visible and accessible every day? If you shop around, you can get a pretty good deal, especially using coupons or Groupons.

STEP 8:
Hang your framed one-of-a-kind family culture board in a high traffic area of your home. This way everyone sees it on a regular basis. This keeps your family culture in the windshield for your entire family.

Consider having a hanging ceremony with your family and a celebration afterwards. By so doing, you are punctuating the value of this with your family.

Use your board as a meaningful reference point for everyone. When praising and reinforcing positive behavior, reference the values on the board as well as when redirecting and setting limits on negative behavior. You have created a document that is etched in the memory of each family member, not to mention friends and extended family who spend time in your home. Think for a minute about the impact the culture board may have on your childrens' friends. As their friends hang out and chill in your home, they too receive a powerful message on what you stand for as a family.

Over the course of time, I encourage you to update your board for a couple of reasons. First, there may be additional values that emerge and you want to include. Second, as your children get older, it is a nice reminder for them and gives you an opportunity for a fun family activity. The fun process of creating your culture board offers your kids a meaningful family memory and a great tradition for them to continue with their future families.

CULTURE BUILDING

By defining your shared vision, positive values, and family blueprint, you have taken important steps in shaping and building your family culture. The significance of documenting these three areas is that it makes it real. Putting it down on paper empowers you in two ways. First, ***you define and post the values that define you***. Second, you have a *living* document that challenges you to be more accountable. By hanging this up in your home, you make it a visible reminder of what you stand for and how you are to be as a family.

DEFINING YOUR SENSE OF NORMAL

Just as all cultures throughout the world have norms on what is customary or expected in terms of behavior, your family culture is no different. Your positive values, shared vision, and family blueprint combine to shape the norms that guide your day-to-day actions. Your family culture determines what is normal for your family. These brief stories illustrate this.

It was a breezy Saturday afternoon. My dad rode along with me as I was collecting the weekly dues from my customers on my paper

VALUES GROUNDED PARENTING

route (back in the day, there was no internet and newspapers were delivered by kids on bikes). One of my customers was a loud, gregarious Greek family who always had some weekend family gathering going on. Whenever I came by their house, I was always greeted with a smile and an invitation to join them for a meal or a game of hoops in their driveway. On this particular Saturday, they invited both my dad and I to join them for a meal. We feasted on some of the tastiest ribs and brisket. Although I was just their paperboy, the value they placed on relationships was an undeniable part of their family culture. The joy in their laughter and on their faces served as a great reminder of behaving our positive values. For them, an important part of their sense of normal was togetherness and sharing with others.

On the other hand, our family culture can also negatively impact us. A few years ago, I worked with an adult client who was struggling with depression and anxiety. She was raised in a high-conflict family where yelling, threatening, and marital fights occurred more days than not. She explained that it was not until she stayed at a friend's house in high school that she realized her family was nuts. In her words, "I thought all families yelled and fought like mine." Unlike the family on my paper route, her family culture dismissed the value of relationships and a healthy sense of togetherness and sharing with others.

As much as you shape your family culture, it also shapes you. It is key that your positive values and family culture remain ***visible***. Here are some practical suggestions for maintaining visibility:

- ☑ During family meals, discuss how the values are being practiced. Talk about your family culture.
- ☑ When reinforcing positive behavior with your kids, be sure to link your praise with the value(s).

- ☑ When setting limits and redirecting negative behavior with your kids, be sure to reference the value(s) they need to practice more.
- ☑ When your kids leave for school, remind them to practice their values.
- ☑ Use sticky notes with reminders of the positive values and put them in your kids' bedrooms and bathrooms.
- ☑ Remind everyone that your entire family has a responsibility to maintain your positive family culture.
- ☑ Have a positive values jar and put a marble in it whenever a family member behaves according to your family values. Once the jar is filled, do a fun family activity, highlighting the joy that comes from your positive family culture.

As you probably can tell, the concept of vision, values, and culture remains as the foundational Pillar in raising values grounded children. Before we transition to the second Pillar, strategies and principles that support your day-to-day-parenting efforts, let's review key takeaways.

SUMMARY AND TAKEAWAYS

- Your family culture provides the norms for you and your children's behavior. Your family culture defines your sense of normal.
- Your family blueprint reveals the plans for how you are constructed as a family.
- Your family blueprint covers important foundational areas like expectations, rules, emotion, intimacy, structure/routine, communication, leadership, decision making, conflict, and discipline.

VALUES GROUNDED PARENTING

- In order to build and fortify your family culture, it needs to be made visible, including:
    - Designing your one-of-a-kind family culture board and hanging it in your home
    - Talking openly and regularly about your positive values. This promotes windshield thinking.

PILLAR II
THE FIVE C's: EFFECTIVE PARENTING STRATEGIES & PRINCIPLES

CHAPTER 4

CONSISTENCY & COMPETENCY: GROWING TRUST & CONFIDENCE

CAN I COUNT ON YOU TO WALK THE TALK? This question is often a silent one that your children ask as they watch what you say and do as parents. The answer has to do with consistency, the first of the five C's. Consistency relates to building trust within your families. It serves to anchor your relationships within your positive vision and values.

Do I have what it takes to make it? Children ask this question as they grow up, highlighting the importance of developing and recognizing their positive qualities, also known as competencies. By knowing what they are good at, your kids develop confidence to engage life more and experience how being values grounded helps them learn, grow, and thrive. In the sections that follow, consistency and competency will be explained in greater detail, highlighting specific ways you can put these concepts into your everyday parenting.

CONSISTENCY

You mean what you say, and you say what you mean. Consistency means implementing your family blueprint daily. It means consistently

CHAPTER 4: CONSISTENCY & COMPETENCY

behaving according to your positive values from morning through night. It means following your shared vision, whether your current family situation is peaceful or turbulent. As a leader within your family, consistency is the fuel that grows and strengthens your family culture.

Consistency is equated with trust. If you want your children to trust you, it is important to consistently walk the talk every day. Consistency leads to predictability. When you are predictable, your kids can count on you to lead and guide them. Your kids see how the positive values on your family culture board are brought to life in your day-to-day actions. As the saying goes, *"I do. You do. We do."*

THE ONE-ARMED BANDIT AND INCONSISTENCY

Have you ever been to Las Vegas? I remember my first time walking into Caesar's Palace. A siren blared, a multicolored strobe flashed, and bells clanged. A hysterical gambler, hands flailing in the air, had just hit the jackpot. Coins were being spit out as if the machine had sprung a leak. She scooped her bounty into this oversized plastic winner's cup. Others looked on in awe, perhaps anticipating that they could be the next jackpot winner!

Other than nickel and dime poker night with the guys, I am not into gambling. I consider myself a fortunate man, though not a lucky one.

On this occasion, however, I thought to myself, heck, why not? Maybe, just maybe, I could be *that* lucky guy. So, I bought 20 bucks' worth of quarters, secured an extra-large winner's cup to hold my anticipated winnings, and cased the Slots O' Fun area for a bloated machine.

After just a few tugs on the handle, I won . . . two bucks. Before I knew it, I was up eight bucks—almost a 50 percent profit from my original investment. Confidence growing, I ordered a cold brew to celebrate my anticipated jackpot. Then, things changed. The payouts all but stopped, and I found my pile of quarters dwindling. As I approached my last couple of bucks, I won again—a buck fifty payout, but the excitement of what could be was fleeting. As I reached down to grab some more quarters, my fingers felt nothing but the cold, plastic bottom of my loser's cup. I was another hapless victim of the one-armed bandit.

So, what do slot machines have to do with being a *consistent* values grounded parent? Well, one of the biggest reasons why people continue to gamble their hard-earned money has to do with a principle called intermittent reinforcement or inconsistent reinforcement. The brains behind the slot machines use a basic, though incredibly effective, behavior principle that involves inconsistently reinforcing a desired behavior. In this case, the desired behavior is gambling or giving the casino your hard-earned money.

Let's switch the scene from Vegas to your home and your kids' bedtime routine. Let's say your family blueprint indicates that your kids' bedtime routine consists of brushing teeth, getting in their jammies, and being in bed by 8:30. What happens if you do not consistently reinforce this routine? Let's say your children beg you to stay up an extra 30 minutes. Symbolically, this is like your child playing you like a slot machine. If you allow them to stay up, you are rewarding their efforts at testing the limits. Much like an excited gambler, you now have an empowered child who will anticipate that limits are inconsistently enforced. This inconsistency not only undermines your family blueprint, but it also fuels power struggles. The bedtime ritual is one simple example, though this concept can be applied to various other family blueprint areas, including curfew, completion of chores, homework, respectful language, accepting feedback, and the list goes on.

Another way of looking at inconsistency is that you are gambling the very values that are designed to help raise your children. Just like the drama on the floor in a casino, with loud noises of winning and disappointments with losing, your family will have a similar type of drama. Tantrums will get louder and longer, and disappointments and power struggles will escalate, leaving you emotionally exhausted and feeling ineffective.

If you are inconsistent in your parenting, the message your children receive is that they need to listen to you and follow the family blueprint only *some* of the time. When this happens, the *some* becomes a **sum**. As a result, you end up paying a considerable **sum** as parents with greater burden, power struggles, and emotional angst. By being inconsistent, you dilute your voice and stance as a values grounded parent.

CONSISTENCY, TRUST, AND GROWTH

The more consistently you align your parenting behavior with your family blueprint, positive values, and shared vision, the more your kids learn they can count on you to guide and direct them in healthy ways. This leads to greater trust and positive intimacy, which helps them feel safe. When they feel safe, they are more likely to take on greater challenges.

The following activity offers an opportunity to examine your degree of consistency as an emerging values grounded parent. As a reminder, complete with your spouse/partner and discuss your responses. If you are a single parent, discuss your responses with a family member or close friend—someone who knows you and your family.

ACTIVITY: ASSESSING AND STRENGTHENING YOUR CONSISTENCY

- Rate the degree of consistency in implementing your family blueprint:

  1   2   3   4   5   6   7   8   9   10
  Mostly Inconsistent   Average   Mostly Consistent

- Rate the degree of consistency in practicing your positive values:

  1   2   3   4   5   6   7   8   9   10
  Mostly Inconsistent   Average   Mostly Consistent

- Rate the degree of consistency in which you apply and follow through with limits and consequences:

  1   2   3   4   5   6   7   8   9   10
  Mostly Inconsistent   Average   Mostly Consistent

- Compare your responses from the above scales. How aligned are you amongst the three areas?

- To what degree do your kids trust that they can count on you to be consistent with the day-to-day routine? With modeling and practicing positive values? With helping them grow up and thrive (shared vision)?

CHAPTER 4: CONSISTENCY & COMPETENCY

> ## ACTIVITY: ASSESSING AND STRENGTHENING YOUR CONSISTENCY
>
> ✎ What areas of parenting are you more consistent in (for example, expectations for school, discipline, positive reinforcement, follow-through with consequences)?
>
> ✎ What areas of parenting are you more inconsistent in (for example, expectations for school, discipline, positive reinforcement, follow-through with consequences)?
>
> ✎ Identify two to three areas in your parenting in which you can stay more consistent.

As values grounded parents, here are some of the key areas to be consistent:

- ☑ Behavior expectations for your children AND yourself
- ☑ Daily structure and routine
    - ✓ Clarify the structure for your morning, afternoon, and evening routine
- ☑ Rules regarding technology and other recreational activities (what is appropriate and what is not)
- ☑ Boundaries, Limits, and Discipline
- ☑ Positive Reinforcement
- ☑ Family Together Time—family dinners, play time on weekends, family meetings
- ☑ Affection and intimacy

Here are some practical suggestions for staying consistent:

- ☑ Have regular family meetings—15–20 minutes (can be over a meal)
    - ✓ Discuss positive values, family rules, changes to any of the routines
    - ✓ Discuss how well your kids are maintaining expectations
- ☑ Use Post-it notes to catch your kids doing things right by following routine and values grounded expectations
    - ✓ Post the notes on bathroom mirror and/or in their sock drawer—everyone likes a positive surprise!
    - ✓ Put a note in their backpack or school lunch
- ☑ When setting limits and boundaries, be sure to follow through. The same applies for consequences, both positive and negative.
- ☑ Admit when you have been inconsistent and make effort to regain consistency—this helps restore trust
- ☑ When life circumstances cause you to change your day-to-day routine, practice ***structured flexibility***. Acknowledge to your family how the life circumstance is causing a change to the routine, implement a new or different structure, and encourage everyone to be flexible in adjusting to the new circumstance(s).

COMPETENCY

Competency refers to a person's positive qualities, skills, and attributes. It is hard to grow up and not know what you're good at. Pointing out positives enlightens your kids about their strengths and positive qualities. It helps them engage life more, overcome challenges, and develop confidence.

CHAPTER 4: CONSISTENCY & COMPETENCY

One way you practice competency is by praising your kids. Praise relates to the age-old psychological principle of ***positive reinforcement***. Positive reinforcement can be defined as giving a positive consequence (for example, praise or a reward) in relation to a desired, values grounded behavior. This is one of the most effective ways of shaping and influencing behavior for everyone in your family.

Think back to your childhood for a moment to a time when you were praised and recognized. Who praised you, why, and in what manner? How did you feel? Now, imagine how your kids feel when you make a special effort to point out their strengths, effort, and abilities.

Praise and recognition lead to feeling valued. ***When your children feel valued, you have reached the HEART or core of the values grounded approach. When kids feel valued and appreciated, they are much more likely to behave in increasingly valuable ways. Essentially, you create a virtuous cycle of positive reinforcement.***

One of the more common and emotionally challenging questions kids ask of themselves is, *"Do I have what it takes to make it—to grow up successfully?"* Pointing out their positive behavior through consistent recognition and praise provides valuable feedback that they ***do*** have what it takes. Developing a competency vocabulary helps equip you with the ability to highlight your kids' positive behavior.

EFFECTIVE PRAISE

Effective praise is centered on ***effort and specific behavior***. This means identifying the specific behavior you are praising and the effort underlying it. For example, when your child earns a high grade on a quiz or test, you might say, "You studied hard and put in a lot of effort to earn that mark . . . good job!" A hug or affectionate shoulder squeeze is a nice punctuation mark.

The difference between praising a result versus the purposeful effort it takes to get the result is that you are reinforcing the process.

When your kids are praised for purposeful effort, especially in adverse and challenging situations, they are more likely to demonstrate that same effort to the point of making it a habit. You are reinforcing grit and toughness in the face of difficult circumstances. Let's do an activity to help you practice your competency vocabulary.

ACTIVITY: LABEL THE POSITIVE

Review the following questions and write down your responses. Try to be as descriptive as possible.

- What is valuable about you as a parent? Identify 2 to 3 positive qualities you have as a parent.
- Now take a moment and think about your children's valuable qualities and strengths. Make a list for each child.
- Take a moment and think about how you recognize and praise your children. How often do you praise your kids? How **consistent** are you with pointing out their strengths?

TAKE THE "THREE-A-DAY CHALLENGE"

- Identify three positive behaviors in each child per day and provide verbal praise. Be sure to link praise with a positive value. For example, "You are doing a nice job of cooperating with your sister; that shows the values of care and respect."
- The Three-a-Day Challenge helps provide balance to the redirection we often do as parents.

CHAPTER 4: CONSISTENCY & COMPETENCY

Here are some practical suggestions for practicing competency:

- ☑ Link praise with positive behavior and values.
- ☑ Identify three positives a day for each family member.
- ☑ Make praise meaningful by slowing down, seeking eye contact, and pausing a few seconds after your positive feedback.
- ☑ Avoid sarcasm when praising.
- ☑ On a sticky note, write down a positive action you caught your child doing and put it on their bathroom mirror.
- ☑ Praise effort and perseverance.
- ☑ After praising your child, take a moment to explain how continued practice of their positive behavior can help grow up (vision).
- ☑ Praise honesty and humility when your children acknowledge their mess-ups while still enforcing consequences.

One last comment about praising purposeful effort. The more consistently you praise your kids' efforts at facing adversity and behaving according to their values, the more you shape and develop your children to stay motivated and engaged in life. You are reinforcing habits of seeking growth and development—the antithesis of complacency and taking the easy way out. These habits will follow them throughout their lives.

SUMMARY AND TAKEAWAYS

- Consistency is equated with trust.
    - The more consistently you follow your shared vision, family blueprint, and positive values, the more your kids will trust your leadership as a parent.

- The greater your kids' trust in your shared vision, family blueprint, and positive values, the more they learn, grow, and thrive.
- Consistency helps reduce unnecessary drama and power struggles.
- Competency relates to the strengths and positive qualities of your children and family.
    - A child needs to know what they are good at in order to grow and thrive.
    - Pointing out positives grows healthy intimacy in your relationships with your kids.
    - Praise purposeful effort and perseverance in the face of adversity.
    - Identify three positives in your children every day and directly verbalize them.
        - When pointing out positives, link your praise to the child's behavior and the value their behavior demonstrates.
        - Avoid shallow praise—this dilutes trust.

CHAPTER 5
CLARITY AND CALMNESS: MAINTAINING POSITIVE DIRECTION & MINDFULNESS

ONE OF THE COMMON MISTAKES parents make is being unclear about their expectations for their kids. When you practice clarity, the third of the five C's, you provide much-needed direction and guidance for your kids and family. Clarity increases your effectiveness when you are redirecting negative behavior AND reinforcing positive behavior.

Speaking of negative behavior, how many times have you lost your cool when your kids have tested the limits? Calmness, the fourth of the 5 C's, helps you stay grounded and cool headed in the midst of stressful parenting situations. In this chapter, clarity and calmness will be addressed in more detail, outlining how to practically apply these principles on a day-to-day basis.

CLARITY

Clarity refers to two separate, yet related parenting principles. First, it refers to clearly defining your shared vision, family blueprint, and positive values. By doing the activities in the earlier chapters, you will have accomplished this. Second, clarity relates to a direct style of communication that helps you effectively manage difficult and challenging behavior.

When practicing clarity, you are providing understandable directives and expectations to your children. This supports a proactive approach to reinforcing values grounded behavior. When it comes to behavior expectations, limits, and discipline, it is important to be direct as opposed to indirect. After all, effective leadership within your family involves providing **direct**ion not **indirect**ion.

CLARITY AND DIRECTION: GOING ON A HIKE

Imagine going for a hike in a densely wooded forest with your family. At the trailhead, you pick up a photocopied map of the hiking trails and set off. After about 45 minutes, your family tells you they are ready to head back. You check the map for guidance. As you study the map, it is apparent that the copy is very unclear. It is next to impossible to make out half the trails—let alone the one you are on. Your kids begin to ask you, "How do we get back?"

How are you feeling in this situation? As a family, what is this experience like? If you answered confused, lost, and concerned, that would certainly make sense.

In the above example, the map serves as a metaphor for your vision, values, and family blueprint. When these three are clearly defined, you are in a much better position to provide direction and guide your children. This type of clarity provides safety and security, growing trust in your relationship with them. As a result, your kids are more likely to follow your lead and direction.

Clarity is only as valuable as it is communicated. This especially holds true when you need to redirect your kids' negative behavior. Using a clear behavioral language can save mounds of unnecessary back and forth debating. Let's look at an example involving clarity regarding problematic behavior.

CLARITY FOR JOEY

Joey was an eight-year-old who threw incredibly loud and raucous tantrums. His parents explained that Joey would "flip out" when they attempted to set limits on him, especially around screen time. They noted Joey would refuse to disengage from the screens, becoming very upset and hot tempered toward his parents. When trying to redirect their son, the parents found themselves in a yelling match with him, telling him to stop or else. It became like a bad script they followed as a family.

The parents noted that expectations around screen use were loosely defined. For example, the rule was that Joey had to be "good" in order to use the computer. The concept of good was not defined in behavioral terms. This left both Joey and his parents at a loss for how to recognize and reinforce such behavior. Additionally, there was a lack of clarity regarding specific guidelines for technology use. Joey seemed to use technology when he wanted and played video games that were inappropriate for his age. If his parents removed the computer, he would find it and sneak it back into his room. This lack of clarity helped fuel the drama and tantrums, leaving both parents and Joey blaming the other and feeling rather frustrated.

We all agreed that establishing clear expectations around screen use was needed. Rather than continuing the bad script of going back and forth, the parents developed a technology contract (see Appendix C for a sample contract). This contract clarified guidelines for technology use and behavior expectations. The proactive language in the contract focused on what Joey needed TO DO versus what he should

CHAPTER 5: CLARITY AND CALMNESS

NOT DO. Consequences for following or not following the contract were clearly defined.

This clarity helped alleviate the back and forth fussing and yelling around screen use. Joey better understood when he could use technology as well as what constituted appropriate use (appropriate games and websites). However, Joey still struggled with accepting limits. His habit of throwing tantrums when being redirected was hard for him to break.

When trying to redirect their son's behavior, the parents often resorted to using an emotional language. For instance, they would say things like, "You're being a brat, stop it," or "I have had enough of your crappy attitude—I am selling the computer!" As you can see, these efforts at redirecting Joey lacked clarity. It was highly personal with no mention of the expected behavior. Without clearly and calmly redirecting Joey to his expected behavior, the consequences became more like threats and punishment.

Maintaining a United Front, the parents pledged to focus their redirection on the expected behavior for Joey. They backed each other up, supporting one another staying calm, firm, and respectful. This shifted the focus to Joey's behavior as opposed to the emotional overreactions. Joey was now afforded greater clarity to step up and take accountability for his behavior. Initially, this was hard for Joey as he was used to blaming his parents for making him mad.

His parents became more consistent in redirecting Joey to follow the technology contract and practice respectful ways of handling his anger and disappointment. The parents used positive reinforcement when Joey accepted the limits and handled his anger with respect. When he did not, negative consequences were consistently applied. Whether consequences were positive or negative, the parents provided emotional support, encouraging Joey to keep practicing expressing his tough feelings in positive ways. This helped Joey understand that limits and boundaries were not personal or designed to be punitive.

With consistent practice and emotional support, Joey was getting better at expressing his feelings in values grounded ways. His parents praised Joey's efforts at being upset in more respectful ways (pointing out an emerging strength or competency). As Joey took greater accountability for following the technology contract, accepting limits and expressing his feelings in respectful ways, the power struggles faded. Joey's self-esteem and confidence grew. Joey was more confident that stressful emotions would not ambush his respect, and his parents were more confident in setting consistent and firm limits.

As the above example illustrates, clarity helped shift the focus to positive behavior expectations. As the parents took the lead, Joey began to follow. Furthermore, you can see how consistency and competency helped within this process. Interestingly, Joey went from feeling ungrateful and upset regarding technology use to a stance of gratitude (4 Anchor value) and happiness for the time he did earn.

Let's do an activity to better understand the value of clarity.

ACTIVITY: ASSESSING AND STRENGTHENING YOUR CLARITY

- ✏ Rate how directly and clearly you communicate behavior expectations for your children:

    1   2   3   4   5   6   7   8   9   10
    Very Unclear   Average   Very Clear

- ✏ Rate how directly and clearly you communicate your shared vision/parenting purpose to your children:

    1   2   3   4   5   6   7   8   9   10
    Very Unclear   Average   Very Clear

- ✏ Rate how directly and clearly you communicate limits, boundaries, and consequences with your children:

    1   2   3   4   5   6   7   8   9   10
    Very Unclear   Average   Very Clear

- ✏ Compare your responses from the above three scales. How aligned are you amongst the three areas? If not aligned, what can you do to bring about greater alignment?

- ✏ Check your responses with your partner and your children. How clear and direct do they experience you in the above areas?

- ✏ Identify two or three specific ways you can communicate more directly and clearly with your children.

VALUES GROUNDED PARENTING

Here are some practical suggestions for practicing clarity (see also Appendix B for additional tips and suggestions on clarity with boundaries, limits, and discipline):

- ☑ Document your family blueprint, including your day-to-day routine, and display it.
    - ✓ Be sure your children are aware of the blueprint and structure.
    - ✓ This has both a clarifying and unifying impact with your family. The greater the clarity, the less confusion, and the more your kids will follow the daily routine.
- ☑ Use your family culture board to clarify your positive values.
    - ✓ Have a family meeting to discuss specific behaviors that demonstrate each value. Ask your children for specific examples at home, school, and with friends.
    - ✓ Be sure to identify behaviors in a proactive fashion. Tell your kids what TO DO versus what NOT TO DO.
- ☑ Be sure your shared vision is clearly defined.
- ☑ Have regular family meetings to clarify behavior expectations.
    - ✓ Be sure to use proactive language (what you want them to do versus not do).
    - ✓ Ask your children to explain back to you their understanding of behavior expectations.
- ☑ When setting limits, use clear, proactive behavior language.
    - ✓ Explain the values grounded behavior you want your kids to practice as opposed to what not to do.
    - ✓ Avoid vague comments/redirects, like "that's enough" or "cut it out." Explain in behavioral terms what you mean so you leave little room for interpretation.

CHAPTER 5: CLARITY AND CALMNESS

- ☒ This not only reduces confusion, but also power struggles.
- ☒ If your child does not change their behavior appropriately, use of a negative consequence will make more sense.
- ☑ Ask clarifying questions.
    - ✓ Can you please explain your understanding of the rules this weekend?
    - ✓ Can you explain what happens if you follow the rules? Can you explain what happens if you don't follow the rules?
- ☑ Adjust your language and words to the age of your kids.
    - ✓ With younger kids, use basic behavioral words, sort of like Dr. Seuss or "Dick and Jane" books.
    - ✓ With teenagers, you can clarify by reminding them of the values and afford them the space and control to fill in the blanks as to how to practice them.

CALMNESS

You know that heightened state of frustration and stress you experience when your kids keep whining and fussing or when your child back talks you? Engaging a state of calmness helps you settle down so your response is not powered by frustration or anger. Instead of back talking your child who just back talked you, you respond with a firm, though calm and respectful, redirection: "Please use respectful words when talking with me and change your tone" versus "You WILL NOT talk to me that way; you are RUDE and ACTING LIKE A BRAT."

Calmness refers to your mood and tone—the state of being emotionally balanced and responsive versus reactive. It implies a sense of peace, mindfulness, and emotional grounding. It does not imply being void of emotion or robot-like. It reflects a healthy balance between the heart and the head.

Remaining calm sets the tone for your child to listen and follow your direction. ***First***, you are creating an emotionally safe environment for your kids to learn and grow. When you stay calm in the midst of your kids' emotional meltdown, you establish a sense of grounding that lets your kids know that you are in charge and will not be defined by the stress of the situation. ***Second***, your calm behavior makes it easier for your children to understand your request and direction. On the other hand, if you lose it emotionally, your kids pay far more attention to your emotion than the actual content of your request to follow your direction.

Practicing calmness involves using a relaxed tone of voice with average volume. Since over 90 percent of communication is nonverbal and para-verbal, calmness helps your words be consistent with your facial expressions, body posture, tone, and volume.

STRESS BUTTONS

For many parents, staying calm in stressful situations is easier said than done. You are on the go most of the time and just the pressure of time is a stressor. More days than not, you are juggling multiple responsibilities in addition to your job as a parent. These demands can be overwhelming, leaving you more prone to overreact versus respond.

Typically, you will lose it when your stress buttons are pushed—we all have them. Your stress buttons can come from past experiences (such as family-of-origin issues or unresolved emotional wounds) and current stressful situations (such as dealing with hyperactive children, defiant kids, work-related stress, whiny and fussy kids, financial problems, and so on).

CHAPTER 5: CLARITY AND CALMNESS

What are your stress buttons? Do your partner and kids know about your stress buttons? The following activity will help you gain greater clarity and awareness of your stress buttons.

ACTIVITY: IDENTIFY YOUR STRESS BUTTONS

Take a moment and reflect on your stress buttons. What do your kids do that push your buttons? What are your triggers as a parent?

- My top three stress buttons:

1. _____

2. _____

3. _____

- When you are emotionally triggered and your buttons are pushed, how do you typically react/respond? What feelings do you experience?
- How can you deal with your buttons so that you respond with actions/behaviors that match your values?
- What are some ways you can model healthy emotional management for your children?

VALUES GROUNDED PARENTING

STRESS & MINDFULNESS: THE CALM THROUGHOUT THE STORM

Under stress, we regress. When you're stressed, your ability to remain calm can easily go out the window. Your capacity to think rationally and identify a values grounded way of handling the stressful situation becomes compromised. Your thinking races, becomes more rigid, and you react—yelling, punishing, threatening.

One parent told me, *"I would not have to yell (at her ten-year-old daughter) if she just listened . . . and didn't yell back!"* Another parent popped his son upside his head, insisting, *"Stop hitting your sister!"* The little fella looked up at him like, *"Huh . . . you're hitting me to get me to stop hitting my sister?"*

So, how do you stay calm in the midst of your buttons being pushed? Since it is not healthy to ignore and suppress stressful feelings, how do you deal with them? Although you can say, "I will keep calm," what does that mean and look like? One approach to staying calm involves this concept called mindfulness.

Mindfulness refers to being aware of the present moment, and being attentive to emotion, thoughts, and physical sensation in a nonjudgmental manner. The concept of mindfulness is by no means a new one. It has been around for many years, most commonly associated with Eastern meditative practices. Research indicates it is quite useful in managing stress and is related to psychological well-being (Keng, Smoski, and Robins, 2011).

Mindfulness is both a process and an outcome. It is a process of being aware of the present moment (circumstances with your kids), your emotion and thoughts related to that moment, and leaning into a nonjudgmental acceptance of your state of being. It is an outcome in how you use the process to guide your behavior.

CHAPTER 5: CLARITY AND CALMNESS

It enables you to see your role clearly and respond effectively. When your buttons are pushed, the goal is to use mindfulness to accept your own feelings and not blame or shame your kids for your frustration, anger, and stress.

It is important to clarify that being attentive to the present moment does not imply passivity. Rather, it is an active process that invites *windshield thinking*. It allows you to be aware of and validate the present stressful moment, and direct your attention to how to respond in a manner that is aligned with your shared vision and positive values.

For instance, when you feel frustrated and irritated at the whining of your five-year-old, mindfulness helps you go from your heart (irritation and frustration) to your head (managing your frustration so you can validate your child's emotions and better understand what might be the underlying reason for their whining). When this happens, the irritation associated with your ego shifts to productive thoughts on how to manage such aggravation in a values grounded manner. When you engage in windshield thinking, you are more likely to behave your values, and your kids are more likely to positively respond.

YOUR EMOTIONAL THERMOSTAT

Mindfulness is like your emotional thermostat. For those who are less familiar with thermostats, these are the little contraptions that are placed on a wall with the sole purpose of controlling the temperature range within your home. Just like a well-functioning thermostat ensures that temperature is within a healthy range, mindfulness helps you establish a healthy range emotionally—not too hot or too cold.

When you practice mindfulness, your brain responds with less activation in the emotional regions that can cause reactive behavior (hot temper). Furthermore, your brain also responds with greater activation in regions that help filter strong emotion, resulting in a more logical and balanced response. The end result: you don't lose your marbles and remain much calmer as parents.

Practicing mindfulness involves engaging your emotion in a manner that invites you to reflect on how you can best deal and cope with it in a calm way. It does not mean that you are emotionally avoidant or sterile, but rather emotionally aware. For those tough-to-manage emotions like betrayal, rejection, anger, fear, disappointment, frustration, and worry, mindfulness helps you seek a balance between experiencing, awareness, and expression.

STINKIN' THINKIN'

Mindfulness also helps you stay calm through awareness of negative and toxic thoughts. Such thoughts can give life to distressing feelings, unseating your calm state of mind. Thoughts like, "*He's doing this to make me mad,*" or "*What she needs is a taste of her own medicine*" can ignite reactive emotion and behavior. These thoughts can easily derail you from your shared vision and positive values—such thoughts are referred to as stinkin' thinkin'. They can lead to ineffective and hurtful parenting behavior, leaving a ***stench*** in your relationships with your kids.

Mindfulness is like the Febreze or Lysol to such negative thoughts. It promotes awareness of these unhelpful thoughts and invites you to shift to fresher, more productive thoughts that are reflected in your shared vision and positive values.

So, what are some ways you can practice mindfulness? Here are some practical strategies and exercises that will help maintain a calm state of mind. It is recommended that you practice these strategies daily:

CHAPTER 5: CLARITY AND CALMNESS

- ☑ Breathing Exercises
    - ✓ 4-7-8 Breathing (Weil, 1999).
        - Breathe in through your nostrils for four seconds.
        - Hold your breath for seven seconds.
        - Breathe out of your mouth, making a swoosh sound, for eight seconds.
        - Repeat four times to complete one cycle.
        - Do three cycles per day: one cycle in the morning, another around noon, and one at night.
    - ✓ Diaphragmatic Breathing/Belly Breathing
        - Sit upright in a chair.
        - Clasp your hands together, put them on the back side of your head, and try to touch your elbows together.
        - While maintaining this posture, take a deep breath in and then exhale. It should feel like you are breathing in your belly.
        - While breathing, think about your shared vision and three positive values you want to practice that day.
- ☑ While driving (home from work and/or picking kids up from school), stream some mindfulness music in your car. Remind yourself of keeping your shared vision and positive values in your windshield when you reconnect with your kids.
- ☑ Get up ten minutes early, engage in some breathing exercises, and meditate on your positive values and shared vision.
    - ✓ When frustrated and angry with your kids, stay quiet for 20 seconds before responding. Practice some deep breathing during the 20 seconds.
    - ✓ Be transparent. Model for your kids that you need to do some deep breathing to stay calm.

VALUES GROUNDED PARENTING

- ☑ Give yourself permission to take a "cool-down." Take five or more minutes to cool down before addressing your child's button-pushing behavior.
- ☑ Remind yourself that it is NOT your child's job to look after your feelings and behave in ways that won't upset you. Tell yourself that it is your job to manage *and* express upset emotion in healthy ways. Remember, you are modeling for them how to handle distressing situations.

Additionally, there are a lot of books and articles on the topic as well as some helpful exercises and activities you can download from the internet. I recommend the following authors: Dr. Shauna Shapiro, Dr. Andrew Weil, and Jon Kabat-Zinn. All three are well studied in the art of mindfulness and offer practical activities and exercises.

By practicing calmness, you are better able to remain focused on your shared vision, family blueprint, and positive values. Mindfulness is the secret sauce that enables you to be responsive versus reactive—to think before acting. When your children are pushing your buttons, calmness helps you to be mindful in managing emotion so you remain values grounded in your response.

Before we move on from mindfulness, I urge you to invite your kids to practice it with you. These practices are just as helpful for kids as parents. More and more schools are using mindfulness to promote well-being amongst the students and faculty, an effort to support a healthy school culture. You can seek out references on the internet for child and adolescent mindfulness activities.

CHAPTER 5: CLARITY AND CALMNESS

SUMMARY AND TAKEAWAYS

- Clarity refers to establishing a clear definition of your shared vision, family blueprint, and positive values.
    - Clarity involves being direct in your expectations, especially when you are setting limits and consequences.
    - Clarity involves using a behavioral language when addressing expectations.
    - Clarity reduces confusion and increases cooperation.
- Calmness helps you regulate emotions so you respond versus react to stressful parenting situations.
    - Mindfulness is a practice that helps you manage strong emotion and stressful life circumstances while remaining values grounded in your day-to-day actions.
    - Mindfulness helps you see clearly and respond effectively.
    - Mindfulness helps you shift from current stressful circumstances and your ego to your parenting purpose.
- Practicing mindfulness helps you identify unhelpful, negative thoughts (stinkin' thinkin') and shift your thoughts to reflect positive, windshield thinking (thoughts about how you can behave in a manner that is consistent with your shared vision and positive values).
- Practicing mindfulness helps keep your emotions within a healthy range (emotional thermostat).
- Breathing exercises can help you stay calm in the midst of conflict and tense emotion.

CHAPTER 6

CONSEQUENCES: SHAPING VALUES GROUNDED BEHAVIOR

CONSEQUENCES REFER TO A RESULT or outcome of behavior—these occur every minute of every day. Some can be quite positive and others rather negative. Whether it be getting an award for student of the week or getting suspended for cheating, both involve choice and an action based on that choice. Some consequences can come and go without much notice, and others can be life altering.

Consequences can serve as a catalyst for meaningful learning to take place. Within the values grounded framework, *consequences are used to teach and instruct.* Whether positive or negative, consequences strengthen your family blueprint, positive values, and shared vision.

Consequences tend to be *most effective* when two things happen:

1. **You apply the consequence shortly after the behavior.**
2. **You are purposeful and mindful about how you apply it.**

Being purposeful when applying consequences is key to helping your kids learn and grow from them. One way you can be purposeful is through the concept of linking.

CHAPTER 6: CONSEQUENCES

LINKING

Linking is a process of connecting the positive or negative consequence to your child's behavior while highlighting the positive value(s) involved.

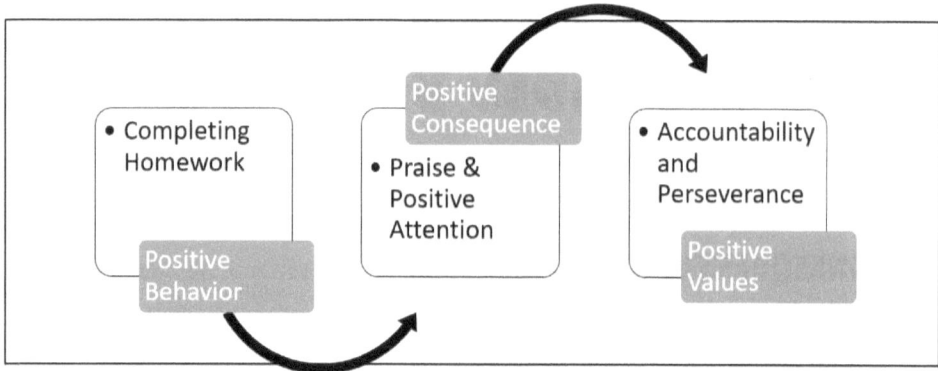

Let's look at an example. Imagine that you are the child in both scenarios. Pay attention to what you are thinking and how you are feeling.

As a 12-year-old, you just completed your homework, including a math assignment that was very tough and challenging.

EXAMPLE 1: *Your mom walks by and comments, "Nice job," and proceeds to the kitchen.*

EXAMPLE 2: *Your mom walks up to you, makes eye contact, pauses a second, and states, "Well done! You put much effort in getting your homework completed, especially your math. That shows perseverance and accountability."*

VALUES GROUNDED PARENTING

In this example, verbal praise was the consequence. What difference did you notice between the examples? How did it feel in the second example compared to the first? As the 12-year-old, did you take away a different message? Note the difference in the parent's statements was probably less than 5–10 seconds. Could you identify how the mom practiced linking?

Let's look at another example. Imagine you are the child in both scenarios. Pay attention to what you are thinking and how you are feeling.

> *As a nine-year-old, you can't wait to eat some of your mom's homemade, scrumptious, chocolate chip cookies. You are told you have to wait until after dinner. After scheming a bit, you sneak a cookie and head off to your room to gobble it up. Your mom walks by your room and notices you are scarfing down the cookie.*
>
> **EXAMPLE 1:** *Your mom walks up to you, wearing a disappointed expression, raises her voice, and exclaims, "What are you doing?! I told you not to eat any of the cookies (she gasps). I can't believe you snuck the cookie. Why don't you listen? That's it . . . you get no dessert tonight!!" She briskly walks out of your room, shaking her head. After she leaves, you proceed to finish eating the cookie.*
>
> **EXAMPLE 2:** *Your mom walks up to you, wearing a disappointed expression, though mindfully and calmly states, "You were asked to wait until after dinner to have a cookie. You chose not to follow directions and your behavior is dishonest. Hand me the cookie (you reluctantly hand over the still warm, gooey cookie). Since honesty is such an important value for you and us as a*

CHAPTER 6: CONSEQUENCES

family, you will receive the following consequences: First, you are grounded to your room until dinner. While in your room, you are to write an apology for your dishonesty, and identify two ways you can practice being honest. Second, you will not have dessert tonight. Let me know when you have finished your apology and two sentences—we will briefly discuss them." She proceeds to walk out of the room.

In the above example, being grounded and removal of dessert was the negative consequence. What difference did you notice between the examples? How did it feel in the second example compared to the first? As the nine-year-old, did you take away a different message? Note that the difference in the parent's statements was probably less than ten seconds. Could you identify how the mom practiced linking? Oh, by the way, the boy sneaking the cookie was me. My mom truly made the best gooey, chocolate chip cookies around!

As the above examples illustrated, there are generally two types of consequences: positive and negative. When used in a purposeful manner, both help shape and influence values grounded behavior. Let's take a look at positive consequences first and then we'll discuss negative consequences.

POSITIVE CONSEQUENCES

As the term "positive" implies, positive consequences involve a desired outcome that is designed to reinforce your children's values grounded behavior. There are a variety of positive consequences, praise being one of the most common and effective.

Consider the word "raise"—it conveys an upward direction. Now, add a "p" (for positive) and we have a great combo! Praise validates your kids' efforts toward growing up (shared vision) and reinforces those behaviors that demonstrate your positive values.

As a general rule, the ratio of positives to negatives should be four positives to one negative.

No matter how old or young you are, being recognized and valued for your efforts and actions is a universal need. In the business world, staff recognition is one of the top, if not *the* top reason, why people remain at their jobs. Your kids' job is to grow up in a values grounded manner. Your praise provides the recognition that they are on the right path. Consistent praise affirms your kids' efforts at behaving according to their values. The activity on the following page explores your personal experience of praise and the impact it has on the relationship with your kids.

ACTIVITY: IN PRAISE OF PRAISE

Think for a moment about when you were praised as a child and/or adult.

- Describe how you felt receiving praise—try to identify at least two emotions.
- Did you replay those positive words of praise later that day... week... month?
- How do you praise your children? What words/actions do you use? How do these words/actions help raise your children?
- How do your kids respond to your praise? What is it like for them to receive your praise?
- What impact does praising have on your relationship with your kids?
- In what areas can you improve with praising your children?

VALUES GROUNDED PARENTING

When I have done training on positive behavior management, there are usually a few parents who ask, "Why should I praise my kid for doing something they are expected to do?" It is a fair and good question. The reason you praise ordinary and expected behaviors is to help shape positive habits in your children. Praising your kids' day-to-day behaviors grows and crystalizes consistency in their values grounded efforts.

For some parents, praising comes relatively easy, and for others, it can be awkward and uncomfortable. If you find it a bit uncomfortable, I encourage you to push through the discomfort. By doing so, you accomplish two things. First, your children will feel valued within themselves and in their relationship with you. This helps grow positive intimacy and closeness. Second, consistent praise helps balance out the redirections, limits, and negative consequences.

CONTINGENCY CONSEQUENCES

In addition to praise, there are other ways to provide positive consequences. When applied in a purposeful manner, material rewards offer an effective and meaningful way of shaping values grounded behavior. ***Contingency consequences*** are rewards when your kids demonstrate a predefined values grounded behavior(s).

Here are some common contingency consequences:

- ☑ Rewards for academic achievement
    - ✓ Graduation present/cash
    - ✓ Cash for above-average grades on report cards
    - ✓ University scholarships for consistent and above-average academic and athletic achievement
- ☑ Allowance for chores
- ☑ Sticker charts, common for younger ages

CHAPTER 6: CONSEQUENCES

- ✓ Potty training—get a sticker for successful toileting. Once there are five stickers, the child chooses a reward.
- ✓ School/academic reinforcement
  - ☒ Positive behavior at school
  - ☒ Completion of homework
  - ☒ School attendance—in the case of a child who struggles with consistent/on-time attendance
- ☑ Behavior plans—target a specific behavior
  - ✓ Compliance with certain rules from the family blueprint
    - ☒ Following nighttime routine
    - ☒ Following morning routine
  - ✓ Listening and respectful language
  - ✓ Self-control

When you think about it, we all participate in and benefit from contingency consequences. Your paychecks are a contingency consequence that positively reinforce consistent attendance, punctuality, and productive work behavior. Employee bonuses are another example of contingency consequences. So, when you use contingency consequences with your kids, you are applying real-world principles to positive behavior management.

BEHAVIOR CHARTS AND CONTRACTS

A couple of the more common contingency consequences involves the use of behavior charts and contracts. Both are documents that identify consequences as related to a child demonstrating appropriate, values grounded behavior(s).

The behavior contract highlights expected behaviors in relation to various consequences. For instance, many parents use contracts to regulate technology use with their kids (see Appendix C for sample). Such a contract typically indicates the time amount per day of technology use as well as specific parameters around use. One parent's contract consisted of the following: His younger children were allowed up to one hour of technology use per day, including weekends. His older kids were allowed 2 hours. Technology use meant any and all screens. Homework needed to be completed and checked before screen time. The parent was the timekeeper.

Consequences were as follows: If screens were used prior to completion of homework and/or the kids did not accept the limits around use, they chose to lose screen time for the next day. Another contingency consequence involved disengaging from the screens.

In order to keep the privilege of tomorrow's screen time, the children needed to respectfully disengage from using the screens—meaning no fussing or protesting. If they protested, they would be given one reminder to redirect their behavior. If they continued to protest, they chose to lose screen time for the next day. This contract was typed up, reviewed during a family meeting, and signed by everyone. Contracts like this can also be developed for other behaviors, such as responsible use of a car, participating in extracurricular activities (need to pass classes in order to play), and so on.

Behavior charts are typically used with younger kiddos. Essentially, they identify a specific desired behavior(s). The parents and the child chart the frequency of the desired behavior per day and/or week. Some parents use stickers or smiley faces as a way of marking the frequency of the desired behavior. Once the child demonstrates the behavior a certain number of times or days, they earn a predetermined reward.

CHAPTER 6: CONSEQUENCES

POTTY TRAINING AND THE BEHAVIOR CHART: AN EXAMPLE

A family sought my help for their four-year-old son who was acting out (throwing tantrums, yelling), mostly around toileting. In particular, this little fella was struggling with the "deuce" or pooping in the pot. He was a pro at peeing in the bowl, especially with the parents putting some fruit loops inside so that he could take target practice.

His parents wanted to enroll him in preschool. School policy required all children to be toilet trained. He really wanted to go to this school because many of his buddies were enrolled and they had an amazing playground.

We all agreed that this problem stunk! We decided to put together a contingency consequence system in efforts to reinforce consistent toileting.

We did a series of interventions to help positively reinforce consistent toileting. First, the parents hung up posters of action figures and cartoon characters, making the bathroom a cool place to sit and hang out. They developed a contingency consequence system where he would earn one sticker for each successful "Number 2" on the potty. On top of earning a sticker for each successful potty trip, the parents doubled down by giving him two bonus stickers for every day he used the potty without accidents (this was to help with consistency). So, *two* bonus *stickers* for *sticking* to the plan of going "Number *2*" in the potty all day!

He and his parents took a field trip to the dollar store and identified a cool fire truck he wanted (cost $3.50). They showcased the fire truck as a reminder of earning his stickers and the value of consistent potty behavior. The parents made a cool, yet simple, sticker chart and their son helped by coloring parts of it.

They were now ready to work the plan. The first three days of the plan were more of the same—inconsistent use of the toilet. He did receive stickers and praise when he successfully used the potty. Then, he put together a consecutive streak of three full days with no accidents. Whoa! He was on a roll.

Every time he successfully used the potty, he ran to his parents (who celebrated with praise, high fives, and hugs), received a sticker, and put it on the chart himself! By the way, these were no ordinary stickers, they were scratch and sniff with a variety of scents that gave him a wonderful smell after he flushed the *"tinky poo."* His three-day streak was followed by a couple of accidents, which was followed by a string of weeks with no accidents. He earned his fire truck, and this served as a wonderful reminder of *"sticking to the plan!"*

Now, let's discuss a few takeaways from the above example. First, the effectiveness of contingency consequences begins with how well they are planned. The parents identified the specific behavior(s) they wanted to reinforce. The plan was clearly (clarity—5 C's) defined BEFORE it was implemented. Second, the parents involved their child in the plan—reinforcing ownership and *accountability* (one of the 4 Anchors). Third, the parents used age-appropriate methods/language of defining and monitoring the desired behavior. Fourth, the parents consistently (one of the 5 C's) stuck to the plan, especially through some of their son's setbacks and accidents. Fifth, the parents provided praise (competency—5 C's) in addition to the contingency consequence, thereby helping their son experience both internal (self-confidence) and external (cool fire truck) rewards. Lastly, this particular contingency consequence had two types of positive reinforcement: a) short-term reinforcement as reflected in receiving praise and a sticker for every successful effort, and b) long-term reinforcement of earning the fire truck and getting admitted to preschool.

The ultimate reward, however, is that this little guy experienced feeling valued by his parents throughout a challenging experience

CHAPTER 6: CONSEQUENCES

of learning a new life skill. The parents rallied around using a values grounded approach as opposed to a reactive one. They disengaged from power struggles around the use of the potty, and he responded by becoming more empowered to use the potty. The tantrums and yelling faded. He now goes to preschool and gets to play with his buddies on one of the coolest playgrounds around!

Also, let's remember that even though their son was inconsistent in demonstrating the desired behavior, the parents did not reduce or take away the contingency reward. When setting up contingency consequences, you want to support your kids' gradual efforts as they work to be more consistent and aligned with their positive values. This is called rewarding *successive approximations.* In the potty example, praise and reinforcement were offered when he made efforts to use the toilet, despite accidents and inconsistent toileting. Although it can be disappointing when your child has a setback, it is key that you maintain your contingency consequence, noting that the pathway to growing up is fraught with hiccups and setbacks. Providing positive consequences through and along the journey is key to reinforcing consistent practice and avoiding the trap of perfection. Removing the reward for a setback would be like your boss taking away your entire paycheck because you were late to work a couple of days.

Here are some practical suggestions for providing purposeful positive consequences:

- ☑ Slow down and make eye contact when giving praise. This makes the experience more meaningful.
- ☑ Smile when giving praise. Doing so adds positive and reinforcing emotion.
- ☑ Provide physical affection—a rub on the back, a high five, a hug. This helps strengthen your relationship and grows positive intimacy.

- ☑ If using a sticker chart or marble jar, hand your child the sticker or marble to place on the chart or in the jar. This action supports ownership for their behavior. Tip: Use colorful and fun stickers and marbles. (I recommend Dollar Store for a good, affordable selection.)
- ☑ Invite your child to help with constructing the sticker/behavior chart.
- ☑ Use linking to emphasize how your kids' behavior demonstrates positive values which in turn help them grow up.
- ☑ Print a picture of the item your child would like for the reward. Cut up the picture into jigsaw puzzle pieces (the number of pieces should be consistent with your contingency plan). Every time your child demonstrates the behavior, they earn a puzzle piece to glue or tape on a blank paper. Once your child earns all the pieces, they receive their reward.

Doing an internet search for "behavior contracts for children and parents" can generate a variety of options from which to choose. Here are just a few to check out:

- ☑ https://www.parentcoachplan.com/printable-parenting-tools.php
- ☑ https://www.understood.org/en/family/managing-everyday-challenges/daily-expectations-child/download-parent-child-behavior-contracts
- ☑ http://www.kidpointz.com/behavior-tools/behavior-contracts/
- ☑ https://www.pinterest.com/pin/405042560214960747/ (sticker charts as well for younger kids)

CHAPTER 6: CONSEQUENCES

NEGATIVE CONSEQUENCES

As the term "negative" implies, negative consequences involve an undesirable outcome. It is designed to redirect behavior that is *not* values grounded or **ungrounded**. Before going any further, let's clarify an important point about negative consequences. The purpose is **quite positive**—even though in the eyes of your kids the outcome is rather undesirable and they don't like it. When applied effectively, negative consequences serve to provide meaningful feedback to your children that their ungrounded behavior needs to change.

Similar to positive consequences, there are effective methods when applying negative consequences. First, when possible, identify the negative consequences beforehand. Include these consequences in behavior contracts (e.g., technology contracts) and when discussing behavior expectations at home and school. Second, explain to your children that, just like in the real world, if they behave in ungrounded ways, they will receive negative consequences. Some of the more common negative consequences include the following:

- ⇨ Removal of a desired activity—loss of privileges (e.g., computer/screen time, play time, dessert, use of car)
- ⇨ Application of an undesirable activity—(e.g., assignments, chores, grounding to one's room)

When applying negative consequences, it is important to use the concept of linking. As discussed earlier, linking involves identifying the ungrounded behavior, the consequence associated with the behavior and the value(s) involved. The chocolate chip cookie example, mentioned earlier, serves as a helpful reference.

Here are a couple of more examples of *linking* with negative consequences:

A 14-year-old who got in trouble with his friends and then lied about it.

I understand you are upset. You are being grounded this weekend for behaving dishonestly. In order for us to trust one another, being honest is important. I understand the temptation of wanting to lie. Hopefully, by being grounded, you will have time this weekend to think more about how to deal with this temptation and the value honesty has in helping you grow up. Here are the expectations: Do a writing assignment on the value of honesty. Explain how behaving honestly helps you grow up and how you can deal with the temptation of lying. No electronics and no time with friends. Again, I understand everyone makes mistakes—use this weekend to learn how you can stop making this mistake—it will help you in the long run.

A 7-year-old who disregarded her parents' request to clean up a mess she made.

You were asked to clean it up three times and chose to continue to play. I understand it is hard to stop doing something you really like and have to clean up, yet that is part of growing up and being responsible. As a result, you have lost your (toy, computer game) for the next day AND you need to clean up.

In order for negative consequences to have a positive effect, it is important to practice consistency, clarity and calmness. Staying consistent means that you follow through with the consequence. This

CHAPTER 6: CONSEQUENCES

strengthens trust in your relationship with your kids as they can count on you to consistently redirect and consequence behavior that is ungrounded. Remaining consistent protects the integrity of your family culture. When practicing clarity, you clearly define the reason for the negative consequences and the specific details involved (e.g., clarify what privilege is lost and for how long). Calmness enables you to keep your focus on your vision and positive purpose and not get sidetracked by your ego or the stressful circumstances surrounding your child's negative behavior. As illustrated in the Joey example in Chapter 5, you can reduce unnecessary drama and protests by practicing these three C's.

When applying negative consequences, avoid making it personal. Remember, your children are still learning and growing and they will make their share of mistakes. Anticipating this will help you be less reactive. On any given day, this can be tough – but just because it is tough does not mean it is impossible or that you can't do it. Keep practicing calmness and give yourself a time out if you get triggered. By remaining calm in the face of frustrating, ungrounded behavior, you will be more effective in applying redirection and negative consequences. Better yet, your children will learn that mistake making is part of life and will be more likely to have a growth mindset.

NEGATIVE CONSEQUENCES: LOVE AND AFFECTION

Communicate to your kids that your love for them is much bigger than their mistakes. This helps them see that grounding them and/or removing privileges does not mean that you love them any less. Rather, the fact that you are taking time out to redirect their behavior is a reflection of your care and affection. Be sure to offer consistent reminders that you love them—though you don't love their ungrounded behavior! Avoid the temptation to withhold love or affection on account of their mistakes. By so doing, you send your kids a "both/

and" message. You love them as valued children and their ungrounded behavior needs to change.

One strategy to help with a "both/and" approach is to separate your child, as a person, from their behavior. That is, they are good kids who have behaved badly. Reminding your children of this allows them to feel guilty for their behavior, but not ashamed for who they are as a person. Shame will shut down your children, whereas guilt enables them to make amends and move on. In Chapter 11, we will discuss in more detail how to use discipline to correct negative behavior without shaming and blaming. Let's take a look at an example that illustrates some of these concepts.

SAFETY AT THE CONSTRUCTION SITE

My son was born to dig dirt and get muddy. He had a passion for construction trucks, bulldozers, not to mention the mere image of a construction site with cones, yellow tape, and blinking signs. As a first grader, one of his favorite things to do was create construction sites in our backyard. He had orange safety cones, "struction" tape, and life-size signage.

One day, he decided to create a "struction" site over by our pool pump. There were live wires and switches that posed a safety issue for my six-year-old boy. He proudly showed me his site, wrapping the pipes in yellow caution tape and securing the perimeter with an orange safety cone. It was quite a site, though it was not safe.

I set a boundary by explaining the safety issue and redirected him to build his "struction" in other areas, but not by the pool pump. I made eye contact with him and crouched to his level as I clarified the safety issue. As we talked about it, he was able to describe his understanding of the safety concern. It seemed like he got the point.

Later that day, I walked out and noticed he was in the early stages of another construction site at the pool pump. A bit concerned, I pulled

CHAPTER 6: CONSEQUENCES

him aside and firmly explained that this was off limits. I added that if he chose to do this again, he would lose his construction cone and tape as a consequence. Again, he looked me in the eye and said "I got it, Pop." I thought to myself, *Okay, that went well . . . he gets the point.*

Fast forward to the following day. It was a beautiful morning, and I went to see what he was up to. Out of the corner of my eye, I noticed the neon orange and bright yellow colors emerging from his "struction" site, smack dab in the middle of the pool pump. The pump and all the pipes were wrapped up in bright-colored construction tape—I could tell he had spent much effort.

I walked back in the house and found him taking a construction break, eating a snack with a cup of juice. He smiled at me, explaining he was hard at work and just needed to take a break. I requested that he walk with me outside and we proceeded over to the decorated pool pump.

When he saw the site and my concerned expression, he made the connection. He started to tearfully apologize, emotionally pleading to let him keep his "struction" cone and tape. I knew he was genuinely sorry. However, as a values grounded parent, I also knew that I needed to follow through with the negative consequence. I knew that following through was important to maintain trust and to teach a purposeful lesson.

After feeling downtrodden for a short while, he rebounded and was back moving dirt piles with his Tonka dozer. Later that week, he was speaking his thoughts aloud, and reviewed with me that he would not play in unsafe areas because it wasn't safe and he didn't want to lose his "struction" tape and cones.

Even though he lost some of his tape and one cone, the situation was a win. It was a win for both of us. A clear boundary was reinforced with a negative consequence that had a positive purpose—safety. He learned the value of listening and respecting boundaries around safety.

It was a good reminder about the importance of following through, even though it was hard to see him so upset at the time.

As a values grounded parent, it is important to anticipate an emotional reaction on the part of your kids, so you do not become triggered and, in turn, either cave by lifting the consequences or overreact by shaming. Rather than judging and applying consequences to them as a person, focus on applying consequences to their behavior. Essentially, you are communicating, "You are a valued child whom I love, though your negative behavior is not valued."

YOUR VITAMIN C

Just like vitamin C helps your body stay healthy, the 5 C's strengthen your parenting so it remains healthy. Each of these principles helps you align your daily parenting with your shared vision, positive values, and family blueprint. The 5 C's reflect best practices in parenting and are essential to raising well-adjusted children. Although each principle applies to a separate aspect of parenting, they all work together to help unify your values grounded approach. The five C's not only make you more effective as a parent, but help grow trust and positive intimacy in your relationships with your children. This makes parenting much more enjoyable.

SUMMARY AND TAKEAWAYS

- Consequences are outcomes to behavior and can be a catalyst for meaningful learning.
    - Consequences work best when they are applied immediately and in a purposeful manner.
    - Linking consequences (positive and negative) to your kids' behavior and your positive values helps meaningful learning to occur.

CHAPTER 6: CONSEQUENCES

- Consequences can be positive and negative; both are used to help support your children behaving in accordance with their values.
  - Positive consequences serve to reinforce continued values grounded behavior.
    - Praise serves as a great reinforcement.
    - Contingency rewards help children experience the connection between their values grounded behavior and earning something valuable.
  - Negative consequences serve to redirect ungrounded behavior.
    - Negative consequences work best when the focus remains on the shared vision, family blueprint, and positive values.
    - Removal of a desired activity or application of a less desired/undesirable activity are two common forms of negative consequences
    - Personalizing your children's negative behavior reduces the degree to which your kids learn from their ungrounded behavior.
- Practicing calmness, consistency, and clarity increases the effectiveness of your consequences.

PILLAR III
BOUNDARIES, LIMITS, AND DISCIPLINE

CHAPTER 7
PROTECTING THE PATHWAY TOWARD GROWING UP

BEFORE BEDTIME, IMAGINE GOING OVER to your front door, turning the knob, and pulling it wide open. Then, you tuck your kids in and get yourself ready for bed. You feel a cool breeze blowing through the entryway as you head to your room to retire for the night. Knowing that the front door is wide open, how well would you and your kids sleep? Other than thinking you were completely crazy, what would your kids be thinking and feeling? How about you? How safe is everyone in your home?

Just the mere thought of an open front door throughout the night provokes all sorts of nightmarish thoughts. From sketchy people who could enter your home to wild, roaming animals and critters, it leaves one cringing. What is it about an opened door that creates such a safety hazard? Simply put, your front door serves as a boundary. When closed, it serves to protect the integrity of your home and the valuable people living in it—not to mention your electric bill!

CHAPTER 7: PROTECTING THE PATHWAY TOWARD GROWING UP

MIGHTY PROTECTORS

Boundaries, limits, and consequences are referred to as the "mighty protectors" as these protect your kids' pathway to growing up. They also protect your shared vision, positive values, and family blueprint. They provide direction and guidance for your children. Let's take a look at the meaning of these concepts.

Limit/Boundary: Expectation of behavior
Consequence: Outcome of behavior, can be positive or negative

To clarify the value of each, let's use the example of a speed limit. These white rectangular signs on the side of most roads identify a clear expectation for how fast you should drive. If you follow the limit, you are more likely to get to your destination safely without an expensive ticket. On the other hand, if you test the speed limit, the consequence can be costly—a possible accident, a speeding ticket, and a hike in your insurance rates. The more extreme your limit testing, the greater the consequence.

What do you think would happen if the police rarely, if ever, enforced the speed limit? How would this impact the way people drive? How would it impact the way you drive? More than likely, our roads would turn into a NASCAR race track—with the drama that comes along with these car races. Without consequences, boundaries and limits are significantly weakened. Consequences *are essential* in supporting limits.

Limits and consequences within your family operate in a similar fashion. You set clear expectations for your children's behavior as reflected in your family blueprint. The greater the clarity (one of the five C's), the more your children understand where the limits and boundaries exist. Consequences are used to reinforce and support these limits, protecting their pathway toward growing up and the integrity of your family blueprint and shared vision.

SWISS CHEESE BOUNDARIES

Imagine boundaries with holes like a slice of Swiss cheese. These are not fully defined or complete. When kids test them, parents allow their behavior to push through. The following is a common example.

Recently, I was at a picnic. As we were setting up, a young girl, about seven years old, was asking her mom for some chips. The mom set a boundary and redirected her daughter to wait 10 minutes until lunch time. The lil' one persisted, testing the boundary, and asked again and again. Her mom responded by giving her daughter a bag of chips. By not enforcing the boundary, the mom undermined her leadership and authority as a parent. By not sticking to the boundary, the daughter learned that boundaries are only partially followed.

After lunch, the mom told her daughter only two cookies. After her daughter ate four, the mom got upset, questioning why her daughter does not listen. The issue was not related to listening; rather, it related to respecting limits and boundaries. The daughter fully understood the mom's boundary, but tested it because she had learned that boundaries are inconsistently reinforced. ***Oftentimes, it is the little tests that grow into bigger ones over time.***

In order to avoid Swiss cheese boundaries, it is key to be consistent (one of the five C's) in your values grounded efforts. In other words, your values grounded parenting approach ought to be 24/7. This increases trust in your relationship with your kids, not to mention strengthening your family culture. Let's look at an example of how boundaries and limits shape kids' behavior.

CHAPTER 7: PROTECTING THE PATHWAY TOWARD GROWING UP

DISNEYLAND, TREE PRUNING, AND SETTING LIMITS

Disneyland is well known for its family friendly atmosphere. Kids of all ages gush with excitement in anticipation of a favorite ride or meeting with their favorite Disney character. The experience is unforgettable.

Our first trip to the family fun park was a blast. After a busy day of rides and meet and greets with Disney characters, we decided to chill out in a shaded rest area. I came upon a Disney crew member, who was pruning some shrubs and trees in the shapes of Disney characters. I struck up a conversation with him, questioning how they managed to shape their plants. He explained that it requires basically two things: 1) a plan for how you want the tree to be shaped, and 2) consistent pruning. He showed me with his clippers that he prunes the branches growing in a downward direction to help the tree direct its energy toward growing in an upward direction. He emphasized that pruning should be done consistently as this makes the task of shaping successful. However, if one is inconsistent with pruning, it is less successful and it becomes a sweaty, time-intensive chore.

So, what does tree pruning have to do with limit and boundary setting?

Well, believe it or not, there are some striking similarities! Much like a landscaper using clippers to help prune and shape a tree, values grounded parents use limits and consequences to shape and guide their kids' behavior.

Just like a tree, children naturally grow in all directions, and their behavior reflects this. In the eyes of children, the world is new and exciting, filled with inviting opportunities for discovery and adventure. Kids *naturally* pursue these new experiences and, in the process, they test limits and boundaries. They rely on their parents to help guide them in a positive and healthy direction.

VALUES GROUNDED PARENTING

Much like pruning downward-growing branches, your job as a values grounded parent is to prune behaviors that cause your kids to grow in a downward direction. Behaviors like disrespectful language, dishonesty, and refusing to accept feedback ought to be pruned. By setting consistent limits and consequences on these downward behaviors, you redirect your kids' energy toward more upward behaviors, like taking accountability for their mistakes, expressing strong feelings in respectful ways, and being honest when tempted to lie. By practicing these upward growing values, their behavior bears new growth and fruit, like rewarding relationships and good grades.

If you are inconsistent with your limits and consequences, it becomes a time intensive chore. Your inconstancy will likely fuel power struggles and unnecessary drama. Rather, if you prune ungrounded and negative behaviors on a regular basis, the work remains constant, though without as much drama, sweat, and angst.

So, how do you decide which behaviors to prune and which to fertilize or reinforce? The answer lies within your shared vision, positive values, and family blueprint. The behaviors that help your children grow up are reinforced (this supports your vision) and those that cause them to grow in a downward direction are pruned. As discussed in Chapter 3, these behaviors ought to be clarified in your family blueprint.

Let's look at a common example that illustrates the value of consistent and clear boundaries.. Brianna is a high-school sophomore and wants to go to Nick's 16th birthday party. Her father asks his daughter who will be at the party. Brianna says a lot of her friends from school along with Nick's parents. The father then explains he would like to meet Nick's parents upon dropping her off. Brianna protests, asserting she would rather die than have her father walk into the party. She pleads with him to just drop her off at his house and not go in.

CHAPTER 7: PROTECTING THE PATHWAY TOWARD GROWING UP

The father remains consistent with the boundary and clarifies that this is not negotiable. He explains that the purpose is not to embarrass, but rather to ensure Brianna will be in a safe place where she can have fun in an appropriate way. Brianna sighs, rolls her eyes, and looks away. The father notes that it is his job (shared vision/positive parenting purpose) to support Brianna growing up in a healthy way. Hanging around a good group of friends and doing fun and appropriate stuff keeps her on the right path. "*Whatever,*" Brianna remarks. As they pull up to the party, the father remains consistent with the boundary, walks into the house, and meets Nick's parents. He briefly checks out the scene to make sure it is a safe environment and that the parents will be supervising the kids all night.

In this example, the shared vision of supporting Brianna growing up in a healthy way was the purpose underlying the limit of going in to meet Nick's parents. Even though Brianna protests, she still gets the message that the limit is about the bigger picture and not meant to be personal.

Years later, Brianna will see that that her father's actions were a sign of love and protection. Using his vision, the father does not rely on Brianna's "five-star approval" for doing what he knows is the right thing. Far too often, parents do not maintain limits such as this one, only to find out that their son or daughter got caught up with inappropriate and unsafe activities.

Linking your shared vision and values with your limits and consequences makes the experience more meaningful for your children. This type of alignment raises the bar for your children to learn, grow, and thrive. This does not mean that your kids will celebrate and like the boundary or limit (typically, I do not receive a thank-you card or a text with a heart emoji from my kids after I set consistent limits). As often is the case, they will understand the purpose *and* the connection between the limit and your positive values as they mature. They will be grateful for your efforts as they become adults.

OUTSIDE IN TO INSIDE OUT

In this section, we will examine the psychological process that occurs with children when you set limits and boundaries. The positive impact of this process will be highlighted. The purpose of limits and boundaries is to go from *outside in* to *inside out*. By setting external limits with your kids' behavior, the goal is for them to internalize the limit (Outside In). As boundaries are internalized, your kids begin to use the limit to guide their decision making and future behavior (Inside Out). The more consistent you are in setting limits, the greater the likelihood that internalization will take place.

For example, let's say a five-year-old boy does not want to share his toys with a neighborhood friend. His parent sets a limit on his selfish behavior, redirecting him to share and be more generous with his belongings (values grounded behavior). In the mind of this little guy, this external limit teaches him that friendships and sharing go hand in hand. The external limit now influences his internal view (decision making) on how he chooses to behave with friends (Outside In). The ultimate goal is for this five-year-old to eventually internalize this limit so he will share on his own (Inside Out), positively impacting his friendships for years to come.

The psychological process of Outside In to Inside Out can be heard from the mouths of our little ones. Oftentimes, we hear young children (typically ages three to seven) engage in self-talk about the limits we set. For example, when setting a limit about not running into the street, we hear our kiddos say something like, *"It is not safe to run*

CHAPTER 7: PROTECTING THE PATHWAY TOWARD GROWING UP

in the street. Stay close to Mommy and Daddy," or in the example above about sharing, "*Sharing toys is what nice friends do.*" This self-talk reflects the cognitive process of children internalizing our boundaries and limits.

Have you noticed that you find yourself setting the same limit over and over again? Hang in there . . . this is common. The process of internalizing boundaries takes time. However, there are several factors that can complicate a child's ability to internalize boundaries. For instance, children who have processing difficulties often take longer to internalize limits. Inconsistent limit setting will also delay the internalization process. A breakdown in co-parenting (problems with a United Front) can dilute the strength of your limits and boundaries. Also, if you do not apply consequences to reinforce your limits, your children will likely see the limit more as a suggestion not an expectation.

USING CONSEQUENCES TO REINFORCE BOUNDARIES AND LIMITS

Let's remember that applying meaningful consequences is key to reinforcing your limits and boundaries. Just like a speed limit sign does little to reduce speeding without police enforcement, your kids will respect your boundaries when they know consistent and purposeful consequences are there to back them up.

Consequences help make the experience emotionally meaningful for kids. As a result, it helps them use these internalized boundaries to guide their external behavior. Let's look at an example that highlights the importance of limit enforcement though meaningful consequences.

A parent came to see me because her children were becoming increasingly defiant and unruly. She was at her wit's end. Her kids did not listen and were driving her crazy. Her teenage son did not pick up after himself, leaving half-eaten meals on the sofa; stinky, dirty laundry on the floor; and his computer games scattered around. To add insult to injury, his younger sister was following in his footsteps..

The mother set clear limits, telling her kids what they needed to do. At the sight of their laziness, she felt compelled to yell, threatening them with no more computer games or play dates. As she yelled, they blew her off, retreated to their rooms, and put on headphones. Exhausted, discouraged, and defeated, she found herself cleaning up their mess with mounting resentment. She was working much harder than her kids.

We discussed that although she set clear limits, she was not enforcing the limits through meaningful consequences. Her yelling and mounting resentment indicated that she was experiencing the emotional consequences of her children's ungrounded behavior and not them. We both agreed that clear, meaningful consequences were needed to redirect their behavior.

We put our heads together and problem solved, and this is what she came up with. If her kids chose to not take responsibility in cleaning up and caring for their belongings, she would pick them up. If she picked them up, she would put them in a sack and donate them to children who would be more grateful for such nice things. The donated items would *not* be replaced. If they left messes around the house, she would hire a house cleaner to come and payment would come through the sale of their computer games and other valuable belongings. The choice was theirs. The big question was, "With this consequence, would they internalize the limit and use it to change their behavior?"

Her kids chose to test the limit, resulting in two bags being taken to a local family shelter. Stunned and in disbelief, her kids watched as their cool shoes, skateboard, computer games, and outfits were donated and not replaced. Initially, her kids protested, blaming their mom for

CHAPTER 7: PROTECTING THE PATHWAY TOWARD GROWING UP

being unfair. She redirected their focus back to them and their ungrounded behavior.

Using the technique of linking, she linked their ungrounded behavior (not cleaning up/picking up after themselves) to the negative consequences (removal of privileges) and the related value(s) (responsibility, gratitude). As they began to see this connection, things changed. Instead of blaming his mom for the loss of his cool stuff, her son internalized the message that he needed to practice greater responsibility in cleaning up for himself; otherwise, more computer games would be donated and sold.

The mother did not use the consequence as a threat, but rather as a simple outcome of their behavior. If they chose to behave responsibly (values grounded behavior), they were able to enjoy the privilege of their wonderful belongings. She would remind them no more than two times to behave in accordance with their values. If they didn't, they understood the emotionally meaningful consequence.

Interestingly, the mother reported that two things occurred. First, her kids listened and followed directions much better. The yelling decreased and arguments nearly vanished. Second, her kids started to develop positive habits and expressed more gratitude for the belongings they enjoyed. The older brother's behavior was now a positive contagion for his younger sister.

In this example, the mom did a nice job of ***linking*** the boundary and consequence with her kids' behavior. Furthermore, she also linked the consequence to their positive values of responsibility and gratitude. When the kids protested the consequence, the mom redirected the focus off of her and onto their behavior. The consequence of donating their items taught the kids a valuable lesson (consequences are designed to teach).

Rather than personalizing your child's protest of the limits, keep your focus on your shared vision and how the boundary will reinforce values grounded behavior. This makes behavior redirection much more purposeful than punitive.

See Appendix B for helpful tips on setting boundaries, limits, and consequences.

SUMMARY AND TAKEAWAYS

- Limit/Boundary = Expectation of behavior
- Consequence = Outcome of behavior, can be positive or negative
- Boundaries, Limits, and Consequences protect your kids' pathway to growing up.
  - These also protect your shared vision, positive values, and family blueprint.
  - They provide direction and guidance for your kids.
- Consequences *are essential* in supporting limits—remember the speed limit example.
- Setting clear expectations for your children's behavior as reflected in your family blueprint is key.
  - The greater the clarity, the more your children understand where the limits and boundaries exist.
  - Use a proactive and behavioral language by telling your kids what you expect them to do versus what not to do.
- Linking your shared vision and values with your limits and consequences makes the experience more understandable and meaningful for your children. This type of alignment raises the bar for your children to learn, grow, and thrive.

- The goal in setting external limits is for kids to internalize the limit (Outside In). As boundaries are internalized, children use the limit and the purpose behind it to guide their decision making and future behavior (Inside Out).

CHAPTER 8

WANTS VERSUS NEEDS: AN EPIC BATTLE AND GROWING PAINS

MOST LIMITS AND BOUNDARIES address an internal battle that happens within all kids. At times, this battle can be fierce, testing limits beyond reason, and can bring parents to the brink of a nervous breakdown. What is this battle? It is a battle of *Wants versus Needs*.

For example, have you ever found yourself telling your child:

⇨ "You've been on the game for hours. Get off the computer. You ***need*** to do your homework."
⇨ "Your room is a mess. You ***need*** to turn off the TV and clean your room."
⇨ "Do not use language like that! You ***need*** to be more respectful."
⇨ "It is getting late. You ***need*** to put away your toys and get ready for bed."
⇨ "We are leaving for school in five minutes. You ***need*** to quit playing around and get ready!"

CHAPTER 8: WANTS VERSUS NEEDS

What is a common reply you hear from your kids?

⇨ "But . . . I don't *want* to!"

As you can see, when setting limits and boundaries, you are often redirecting your kids on what they **need** to do. Conflict arises when children push back, asserting what they want to do instead. At the heart of this battle is a developmental drive for your children to mature. Maturity is a wonderfully messy process!

As much as kids seek to grow up, it is tough for them to take on more responsibility and behave in accordance with their values. There is an ongoing temptation to take the path of least resistance, do a halfway job, or avoid responsibilities altogether. When this happens, someone typically steps into their lives and directs them to do what is needed. These "someones" are usually you, as well as teachers, coaches, and others who expect your kids to behave according to their values.

When children protest limits and boundaries, it is often fueled by a desire to keep doing what they want. When redirected from their wants to needs, they can feel slighted and stressed. Many kids make it personal, seeing the boundary as a form of rejection from doing what they want.

Think about when you redirect your child to stop playing on their computer and start their homework. What is their response? Do they test the limit and make it personal?

You may have heard outbursts like, "NO . . . leave me alone, you're not fair!" or "This sucks!" or "What's your problem? My friends' parents let them play." These emotionally charged outbursts demonstrate the discomfort children feel when going from wants to needs.

VALUES GROUNDED PARENTING

The process of maturing involves going out of their comfort zone and engaging life in more responsible and independent ways. Whether it be learning to potty on their own, dealing with peer pressure, or doing schoolwork, children are faced with challenging opportunities to do what is needed versus what they want to do.

Growing pains emerge as children engage the battle of wants versus needs. Much like achy joints and bones during a growth spurt, the frustration and angst that come along with emerging maturity represent their own set of emotional growing pains. Power struggles, arguments, and persistent fussing can reflect these growing pains.

Many parents also struggle with growing pains. As your children mature, you are learning the difficult balance between guiding them and letting them learn on their own. This reflects a wonky process, leaving parents confused, frustrated, and concerned. Just like your kids, ***you mature as parents as you grow along with them***. Increasing awareness around growing pains can be quite useful. The activity on the following page will help with this.

CHAPTER 8: WANTS VERSUS NEEDS

ACTIVITY: MATURITY AND GROWING PAINS

Think for a moment about what your experience of maturing was like.

- What was the battle of wants versus needs like for you as a child?
- What valuable mistakes did you make? What were some of your growing pains? What did you learn from them?
- How did your parents support your emerging maturity?
- As a parent, how do you balance your wants versus your needs?

Hold a family meeting and talk with your children about the wants versus needs battle. Explain the concept to them and discuss the value and challenge in balancing their wants versus needs. This activity can be done with kids as young as five or six all the way to young adult children. Talk about the challenges of doing what is needed (responsibility) versus what they want to do (fun, pleasure). Explain how this relates to maturity. Discuss ways that you can support and encourage their emerging maturity so power struggles are minimized.

- What positive values can they practice to help strengthen their emerging maturity?

LEARNING THE LANGUAGE OF EMOTION

As many of you already know, the battle of wants versus needs gives rise to all sorts of hot-blooded emotions. Teaching your children emotional management skills will help them mature and endure this battle successfully. Keep in mind that learning to express emotion is like learning a new language. It takes time and ongoing practice.

A common mistake we make as parents is assuming that our kids should know how to express vulnerable feelings like disappointment, sadness, anger, hurt, rejection, confusion, and worry.

Developing emotional awareness and establishing an emotional vocabulary is a process that takes time and ongoing practice. Your children need your patience and support as they seek to learn these emotional management skills. Mirroring your children's feelings is a great way to teach emotional awareness and expression. As the term implies, mirroring is a reflective process that highlights your child's feelings. It involves making empathic statements like, "You look sad," "I can see you are very upset," or "I wonder if that scared you?" These statements help your child identify and label their feelings. Consistently encouraging your children to express their strong feelings using respectful words, gestures, and behavior helps build their emotional management skills. Mirroring not only validates your child's emotion, but it can generate meaningful conversation about their feelings and ways to manage them.

This process, however, is not easy. Most children feel vulnerable when sharing their emotions. Children need to feel heard and understood. In sharing their feelings, they are taking a risk by trusting you to

CHAPTER 8: WANTS VERSUS NEEDS

listen and understand. Active listening and mirroring are ways you can listen without judging them.

As your kids become more aware of their emotion, it is important to encourage them to label and express their feelings. Using words to describe emotion helps make an abstract experience a bit more concrete for your kids and you. Furthermore, it helps your kids seek and receive support in times of need.

When you take time to listen to your children's feelings, you are communicating to them that they are valued—a hallmark of values grounded parenting. Compassion, empathy, and concern are great values for your kids to experience through your actions.

Remember that children are not born with a skill set on how to express their feelings, especially strong and stressful emotion. They rely on you to be patient and supportive as they practice their emotional management skills. Your kids will make mistakes as they learn this valuable skill. When feeling hurt, they may say hurtful things. When angry, they may say or do things that make you angry. This can make it hard for you to empathize with them. In the next chapter, we will discuss an approach that helps you validate emotion while redirecting negative behavior.

Here are some additional tips in helping your children with emotional expression:

- ☑ Model healthy emotional expression for your children.
    - ✓ During meal time, talk about feelings as a family—take the lead in sharing.
    - ✓ Demonstrate respectful behavior when expressing your feelings.
    - ✓ If you get triggered, take a cool down.

VALUES GROUNDED PARENTING

- ☑ Use a feelings chart to help your kids identify and label their feelings.
    - ✓ If you do a search on the internet, you can download free charts or purchase them at an affordable price. There are charts for children at different ages.
    - ✓ Ask your child to use the feelings chart to identify and label their emotion.
        - ☒ Encourage your child to identify multiple feelings. This not only helps expand their emotional vocabulary but also teaches them that you can feel multiple ways in a given situation.
- ☑ Teach your children that feelings are neither right nor wrong.
- ☑ Actively listen to your children's emotions.
    - ✓ Be patient as they try to find the words to express what they're feeling.
    - ✓ Validate that it is sometimes hard to find the right words to express such complicated emotion.
    - ✓ Remind your kids that putting strong feelings into words is hard—though just because it is hard does not mean it is unhealthy or wrong. They should continue to practice as this will help them have happier and stronger relationships.
    - ✓ Do not shame your kids when redirecting their mistakes. Shame often silences children—a silent child internalizes their feelings, which can stunt their process of growing up.

PROTECTING THE RELATIONSHIP WITH YOUR KIDS

Given that the battle of wants versus needs happens in all children and families, it is important to protect your relationships from the emotional fireworks that often occur within this conflict. One way to do this is to lean into your Anchor value of humility and not let your ego and pride get in the way. Remember to be patient throughout this process as your kids are learning as they are growing. Setbacks, although discouraging, reflect growing pains and are part of the maturity process.

Your children need you to be empathic and understanding as they fight this internal battle. They need your support and validation that you will have their back as they struggle with doing what is needed versus what they want. Being empathic and understanding does not mean you water down your boundaries and consequences when negative behavior surfaces during their battle. Rather, it involves a both/and approach. You validate your child's emotion and set a firm, clear boundary on their negative behavior. Remember to stay connected to your shared vision, focusing on the positive purpose behind the boundary and not the snarky outbursts that may be evoked by it.

> **Keep in mind that the battle of wants versus needs is ongoing with children/teens as they grow up. The temptation to take the easy way out is always lurking. Be battle ready with a respectful, supportive, yet firm stance to support your child taking the right course and practicing values grounded behavior.**

SUMMARY AND TAKEAWAYS

- The process of maturing involves going out of one's comfort zone and engaging life in more responsible and independent ways.

- Maturity involves kids doing what is needed versus what they want—the conflict between wants and needs occurs in all kids.
  - The battle of wants versus needs is ongoing—not a one and done battle.
  - Just like children, parents have growing pains as well.
  - There is an ongoing temptation to avoid responsibility. Most humans, not just kids, grapple with taking the path of least resistance.
  - Boundaries, limits, and consequences help them move beyond the habit of taking the path of least resistance.
  - Children often personalize boundaries, limits, and consequences as rejection of their wants. The process of maturing is emotional for both children AND parents.
- The wants versus needs battle brings up hot-blooded emotions in your children.
- It is important to teach and support healthy emotional expression.
  - Mirroring and active listening help your children feel heard.
  - Mirroring and active listening grow positive intimacy and closeness.
  - Teach your kids healthy emotional expression through modeling it yourself.
  - Find opportunities to talk about feelings and reinforce your children's efforts.
  - Empathizing with your children's emotion helps them feel valued.

CHAPTER 8: WANTS VERSUS NEEDS

- Teaching and reinforcing healthy emotional expression is a valuable skill that helps kids learn, grow, and thrive.

It is a "both/and" approach to being attuned to your children's feelings and reinforcing healthy ways they can express themselves.

CHAPTER 9

THE VPC: APPLYING EFFECTIVE LIMITS AND CONSEQUENCES

SETTING EFFECTIVE BOUNDARIES and consequences is one of the harder challenges parents face. Children often perceive that limits and negative consequences keep them from doing what they want. Many kids personalize limits, experiencing them as a form of rejection. This evokes protests of all kinds, leaving parents exhausted, frustrated, and wondering "Are they ever gonna get it?"

When parents get worn out and frustrated, they find it more difficult to be emotionally attuned and supportive to their kids, especially when they are testing the limits. As a result, loving parents can shift from an emotionally comforting stance to one that is emotionally dismissive. Such parents may find themselves saying, "I don't care if you're tired, you need to clean up NOW!" or "Why are you so mad? ... It's not that big of a deal ... just do what you've been asked."

If you are like most loving parents, you want to set limits without the back and forth yelling and tug of war protests. You don't want to dismiss your child's feelings, and you want them to respect your boundaries. You want to be loving and firm. In this chapter, we will discuss an approach that helps you do just that.

CHAPTER 9: THE VPC

The Validate, Promote, Consequence (VPC) approach is a "both/and" strategy to limit-setting. It involves a way of interacting with your kids where you are attuned to your child's feelings and, at the same time, reinforce healthy ways they can express themselves. By using the VPC, you are able to BOTH validate your child's emotions AND redirect their limit testing behavior.

The VPC stands for:

Validate
Promote
Consequence

Let's take a look at what each of the three concepts means, and then specific examples will illustrate what this strategy looks like in real life.

VALIDATE

Validate refers to affirming your children's emotion and experience. It helps them feel heard and understood. Validating helps you stay emotionally attuned to your kids as you set limits and redirect their behavior.

> **When you validate, you are affirming your children's feelings and experience. You are not validating their negative behavior.**

This is a key difference and one that will help you maintain a strong relationship with your children when you need to set limits and consequences.

Here are some examples and tips to help with validating:

- ☑ Take the perspective of your child; put yourself in their shoes (even if you feel they are overreacting, try to imagine their feelings and perspective).

- ✓ Taking your child's perspective helps show empathy.
- ✓ Perspective-taking grows trust and positive intimacy.
- ☑ Remember that *validating is not necessarily agreeing* with their perspective and/or validating their behavior. It is affirming their feelings.
- ☑ Express your validation in words to your child. For example:
  - ✓ "I see you are quite upset, and I want to hear your side."
  - ✓ "I sense this is difficult for you."
  - ✓ "I get it . . . what your sister said really upset you."
  - ✓ "I want to hear what you have to say because it is important."
  - ✓ "I see you are very frustrated. What you have to say is important, and I would like to hear your side."
- ☑ If you are triggered, take a brief cool-down for yourself. As noted earlier, stress can block your ability to be emotionally attuned to your kids' feelings.

PROMOTE

Promote is about promoting and encouraging values grounded behaviors to replace ungrounded or negative behaviors. Promoting is leading and directing your kids regarding what you expect them to do.

Pro = Forward
Mote = Motion

When you promote, you are encouraging your kids to make forward motion toward a more positive behavior.

One of the common mistakes you can make in limit setting is redirecting your kids on what NOT to do versus what TO DO. The reason why this is ineffective is it redirects your kids toward an absence of behavior as opposed to a more functional and values grounded behavior.

Let's look at an example that illustrates this. In the scenario below, a nine-year-old is poking and aggravating his seven-year-old sibling in the car. The following process unfolds:

> **Parent:** "Don't poke him."
>
> **Older Child:** (*He stops poking, and now is flicking him.*)
>
> **Younger Child:** "STOP IT!"
>
> **Parent:** "I just told you to stop it! Cut it out!"
>
> **Older Child:** "But I am not poking him."
>
> **Parent:** "That is enough! I have had it."
>
> **Older Child:** "But he likes it."
>
> **Parent:** "What makes you think he likes it? You are annoying him."
>
> **Older Child:** (*He gives his brother a wet willy [wets his finger and puts it in his brother's ear].*)
>
> **Younger Child:** "MOM, he put spit in my ear!"
>
> **Parent:** "That's it, you're grounded."
>
> **Older Child:** "Why? I did what you asked . . . I stopped poking him."

Although the parent was trying to set limits, she told him what not to do (don't poke him). As we see, the son followed his mother's limit, only to engage and seek attention from his brother in another way (flicking). This was followed by a generalized comment of "I just told you to stop it! Cut it out!" These general redirections are typically ineffective as

VALUES GROUNDED PARENTING

they do not direct the child toward a more functional behavior.

Furthermore, when it comes time to provide a consequence, either positive or negative, the parent has not identified a specific behavior to attach to the consequence ("stop poking your brother" is an absence of behavior). This lack of clarity compromises the effectiveness of both limits and consequences, leaving all involved to feel frustrated.

Let's look at the same example, this time with the parent redirecting and promoting a more functional behavior.

> **Parent:** "Keep your hands to yourself and respect his boundaries."
>
> **Older Child:** (*He leans into his brother with his shoulder.*)
>
> **Younger Child:** "STOP IT! . . . Mom, he's hitting me with his shoulder."
>
> **Parent:** "You have been asked to respect his boundaries. That means not touching him and staying out of his personal space. Are we clear?"
>
> **Older Child:** "Yeah . . . you guys are no fun."
>
> **Parent:** "How about a game of who can make the silliest and grossest face?"

In this example, the frustration was nearly absent. The parent redirected the older son by promoting a more functional and values grounded behavior (hands to self and respecting boundaries). As kids often do, he tested the boundary and his mother remained consistent, proactive, and clear with her behavior expectations. Also, notice how she redirected the older boy's attention-seeking behavior with a more age-appropriate way of engaging his younger brother's attention (making silly and gross faces).

Now, many of you may wonder, "What if the older child did not follow the parent's redirect and continued to aggravate and poke his older brother?" Consistent with the VPC model, a negative consequence will be provided. Such a consequence may include spending some time in his room and doing a writing assignment on the value of respecting boundaries. The experience of spending 30 minutes in his room allows him the space and time to process the value of boundaries and respecting them. Before covering consequences, let's review some practical strategies on promoting.

Here are some tips for Promoting:

- ☑ When redirecting negative behavior, ask yourself, "What positive behavior do I want to see from my child?"
- ☑ Use a measured, clear, calm, and firm tone of voice. Be brief and to the point; too much talking dilutes your request.
- ☑ Use behavioral language when promoting replacement behavior.
    - ✓ "Please sit quietly."
    - ✓ "Please keep your hands to yourself."
    - ✓ "Please take turns with your brother."

Here are some examples of a parent using both Validating and Promoting. Notice how the parent promotes a clear direction for the child:

- ☑ "I see you are upset right now. What you have to say is important. Please lower your voice so we can talk about it."
- ☑ "I understand that math is frustrating for you. Please take a moment to calm your mind, and let's see if we can figure it out together. I know you can do this (sprinkle in some encouragement)."
- ☑ "I understand that you do not want to go bed, especially since you were enjoying the game so much. You can play the game tomorrow if you like. Please stand up and walk to the bath-

room so you can brush your teeth."
- ☑ "I see that you are angry. I am not asking you to stop being angry. I am asking you to be respectful AND angry. Please change your tone so that it is more respectful."
- ☑ "I understand you are upset with me. I can see why you would be upset with me. Please take a moment to calm down by lowering your voice. Then we can try to talk about this in a good way."

CONSEQUENCE

As noted earlier in Chapter 4, consequences are outcomes to behavior and can be either positive or negative. The purpose of consequences is for teaching and learning; the ultimate goal is to reinforce values grounded behavior. Your aim is to provide a four-to-one ratio of positive-to-negative consequences.

It is important to not only reinforce exceptional and outstanding behavior in your kids (solid report card, great performance in music, sports, art, and so on), but also the everyday, ordinary values grounded behavior that helps them grow (getting to school on time, completing homework, doing chores, cooperating with siblings, using respectful words, trying healthier and different foods, and so forth.). Every time you praise your kids for their values grounded behavior, you are affirming their efforts toward growing up AND they are more likely to continue these positive, values grounded behaviors.

Consequences provide the reinforcement that strengthens and supports your boundaries and limits. Remember the speed limit example. Without consistent enforcement of the speed limit, the signs would be merely a suggestion.

CHAPTER 9: THE VPC

Here are some tips on use of consequences:

- ☑ Provide four positive consequences for every one negative consequence.
- ☑ Make negative consequences about the behavior and NOT the person—"Your behavior is bad" versus "You are a bad kid."
- ☑ Stay focused on your family culture and reinforcing the positive values when providing consequences.
- ☑ BE MINDFUL and thoughtful when using consequences, especially negative consequences.
  - ✓ Avoid setting consequences when you are angry and distressed. Calm yourself first.
  - ✓ When you are calm, you are less likely to personalize your child's negative behavior.

The following examples illustrate the VPC approach. Additionally, these examples connect the dots with other important values grounded principles mentioned earlier.

EXAMPLE 1: A 12-year-old is having to do her homework. Her parent uses the VPC to support this process.

You are putting a lot of effort into your homework today. I imagine that is not easy after a long day of school (Validate). Stay strong and keep focused to complete your work neatly (Promote). Your behavior shows persistence and accountability—two wonderful values that help you grow up! (Linking). If you keep this up, you will have even more time to play with your friends this afternoon (Positive Consequence).

VALUES GROUNDED PARENTING

EXAMPLE 2: An eight-year-old protests and yells after being told to stop playing and get ready for dinner. The parent uses the VPC to address the verbal/emotional outburst.

I see you are upset. It is hard to stop playing a game you like (Validate). Please lower your voice. Remember the rules we discussed around playtime and dinner (family blueprint). I am not asking you to like it, and you need to get ready for dinner. This means quietly going to wash up and then coming to the dinner table (promote). It is quite all right for you to be upset . . . and get ready for dinner (both/and).

Thank you for following directions. I imagine it is not easy to stop doing what you want and do what is needed (Wants versus Needs). You did a nice job of being upset and doing the responsible thing (Linking).

EXAMPLE 3: A 13-year-old wants to go to a friend's house to play. He is trying to avoid doing his homework before he goes (Wants versus Needs).

Before you go to James's house to play, your homework needs to be completed. I understand that James has a cool new game (Validate) AND your homework needs to be completed before you go (Promote). Remember, the value of taking care of your responsibilities and work before you play (Linking).

Well done. You completed your work and now you can go over to James's house (Positive Consequence).

CHAPTER 9: THE VPC

EXAMPLE 4: A 16-year-old decided to go to the movies (past curfew) without checking with her parents beforehand. The parent uses the VPC to apply negative consequences and support the family blueprint (behavior expectations).

I understand that you simply forgot to call and ask if you could go to the movies. Mistakes happen (Validate). Although you think it is silly to have to call, check in, and ask if you can go to the movies (Validate), the rules are there for a reason—safety and respect (Linking). As you know, the expectation is for you to call and ask to go to the movies (Promote). As a consequence, to help you remember next time, you will be grounded the rest of the weekend without use of your phone. During this time, I hope you will think about the importance of respecting the rules, even though they seem silly.

EXAMPLE 5: An 11-year-old slugs his 10-year-old brother for taking his game without asking. The parent uses the VPC to address the son's anger and aggressive behavior.

I understand that you are very angry with your brother, especially since he took your game without your permission. I understand the feeling of wanting to slug him. It is wrong for him to take without asking. I will address this with him (Validate). However, hitting is not okay . . . not in our home or elsewhere. Hitting is hurtful and is not a healthy way of showing anger. It creates more problems. When feeling like you are going to hit or push, you are to walk away and/or ask for help (Promote). It is your job to practice self-control, as hard as it can be at times. Self-control is a tough but very important value to help you grow up the right way (Linking with Shared Vision). As a consequence, you are grounded for the remainder of the weekend. During this time, you are to think about and write down how you will express your anger and hurt in respectful ways. Also, you are to apologize to your brother for hitting him. You are not apologizing for being angry with him as you had good reason. Please know that your brother will receive a consequence for taking without asking.

EXAMPLE 6: A 14-year-old stands up for a friend, after hearing others gossip and say negative things behind his back. The parent uses the VPC to affirm healthy boundary setting in keeping positive friendships.

That is a tough situation with your friends, and I can see how it bothered you that they were teasing Joan behind her back (Validate). By speaking up, you set a nice boundary with them, letting them know that it is not cool to talk behind someone's back, especially your friend (Promoting). Your actions show integrity and respect, values that make friendships grow! (Linking). How about having Joan over this weekend and I will spring for some pizza? (Positive Consequence).

As the above examples illustrate, the parent engages a "both/and" approach, helping their child feel validated and heard while also reaffirming their boundaries. Positive and negative consequences were used to reinforce values grounded behavior in their children. The technique of linking was also applied to help their children make the connection between their behavior, the consequence, and positive values.

ONE AND DONE ASSUMPTION

One of the mistakes parents can make is the *one and done assumption*. This assumption states that if you have talked about it once, your kids should know better and the issue should be done. Certainly that would be nice. ***However, going from wants to needs is not a one and done process.*** Rather, it takes time, rehearsal, and practice, even the routine behaviors like getting ready for bedtime, curfews, chores, homework, and so on.

Every time you use the Validate, Promote, and Consequence approach, you are making your positive values more visible. Remember, the more visible your values become, the stronger your family culture. When promoting values grounded behavior, you are also inviting your children to engage in windshield thinking. As a reminder, windshield thinking involves your kids thinking ahead for themselves and seeing how their values help them grow up and mature. Imagine the value this has when your kids are ready to leave home and engage the world on their own. Their vision is colored by these positive values and a history of practicing such values.

A reference guide of practical strategies and tips for setting limits, boundaries, and consequences can be found in Appendix B.

SUMMARY AND TAKEAWAYS

- The Validate, Promote, and Consequence (VPC) model provides a means to reinforce positive behavior AND redirect negative or ungrounded behavior.
- The VPC involves a "both/and" approach that allows you to be attuned to your child's perspective/feelings and reinforce healthy ways for them to express themselves.
- Validating means affirming your children's feelings and experience. ***By validating, you are not affirming negative/ungrounded behavior.***
- Promote is a proactive way of identifying the positive, values grounded behavior you want your children to practice.

VALUES GROUNDED PARENTING

- Tell your kids what TO DO versus what NOT TO DO.
- Consequences support/reinforce values grounded behavior.
- It is important to positively reinforce not only exceptional and outstanding behavior (accomplishments and achievements), but also everyday, ordinary values grounded behavior that helps your kids grow in an upward direction (consistently completing homework, being ready for school on time, respectful language, etc.).
- Every time you praise your kids for their values grounded behavior, you are affirming their efforts toward growing up.

CHAPTER 10

BOUNDARIES, LIMITS, AND CONSEQUENCES WITH TECHNOLOGY

IT WAS A BEAUTIFUL SATURDAY MORNING, and we went out for breakfast. My family decided to go to a place just down the street that happens to be the mecca for blueberry pancakes. Silliness is one of our positive values—one that we practice naturally! So, we started cracking jokes, and scheming ways that we could bust the server's chops when ordering our food.

We were seated next to a family of four with two teenagers—similar to our own. I could not help but notice that this family was fully engaged on their electronic devices. It was odd in a sad way—conversation was nearly absent. The silence that surrounded them spoke volumes. Even though they were seated close to each other, they seemed miles apart.

After scarfing down our delicious breakfast, making a few more wisecracks, it was time to go and engage the day. As we got up to leave, I noticed the postures of that family had shifted—they were now turned away from one another, heads down and focused on their screens. What a bummer and lost opportunity! Instead of communicating and connecting with each, they were more intimately connected with their electronics.

CHAPTER 10: BOUNDARIES, LIMITS, & CONSEQUENCES WITH TECHNOLOGY

Undoubtedly, we are in the midst of a technological revolution, and many parents struggle with balancing technology and family time. After all, it's not just the kids that are consumed with electronics, but parents as well. Technology and the irresistible screen present a unique set of challenges for today's parent.

I am using the term technology broadly as there are so many applications that captivate the attention of children and their parents. There is gaming, social media, videos, websites, streaming, and much more. The purposes of technology go beyond recreation and entertainment. Many schools and companies use technology as a valuable teaching tool. Technology is a medium or a platform that informs, entertains, connects, and teaches.

The degree to which people are immersed by the mighty screen makes one wonder if indeed they are in a hypnotic trance! I remember many a day coming home and seeing my kids on their screens. My effort to engage them with a simple "Hi, how are you?" was met with silence and a mesmerized gaze toward their screen. I could not help but question whether their screens carried more value than a live human—not to mention a live human who happens to be their dad! I imagine my mug was nowhere near as interesting or captivating as the social media site or game they were engaged in at the time. With that said, there is a significant principle that needs to be clarified.

Face-to-face, human connection is far more valuable and healthy than engaging with a screen.

Don't just take my word for it; a good number of Silicon Valley executives regulate their kids' use of the very technology that they spend their careers developing! They recognize the addictive nature of today's technology and maintain strict limits for their children. They also recognize the value of face-to-face connection and how screen time can interfere with meaningful social relationships.

As you might surmise, one of the reasons that it is so difficult for your kids to disengage from their screens is that the programming is incredibly reinforcing. It is reinforcing emotionally and biologically. While engaging the screen, your kids' brains are being stimulated by all sorts of images that provide irresistible invitations to further engage and stay connected. Their brains release neurotransmitters (e.g., dopamine, serotonin) that are emotionally reinforcing. These brain chemicals can be viewed as a sort of "brain candy."

It is becoming more and more common for parents to seek family counseling due to their children's severe behavior after being told to disengage from their screens. Parents have described heated battles in their home over screen time, characterized by profanity-laced arguments, threats of harm, and colossal tantrums. On extreme occasions, parents have reported that their children have threatened suicide if the parent unplugged the computer.

Perhaps, some of the power struggle over screens and computer time relates to a larger power struggle between the culture you seek to cultivate in your home and the culture outside your home. The value of social connectivity and the impact it has on emotional and social well-being is key to healthy development and happiness. At the same time, technology certainly has benefits and is an essential part of our day-to-day work.

The challenge lies in striking a healthy balance between your family culture and the technological culture. Boundaries, limits, and consequences help you develop and protect a healthy balance.

How do you establish a balance between technology and your values grounded family culture? The first step is to go to your shared vision and positive values. Remember, your shared vision is the centerpiece for all your parenting decisions, and your positive values help you accomplish your vision. The four Anchor Values of accountability, respect, humility, and gratitude, along with other positive values will help you clarify (one of the five C's) a healthy balance.

In the spirit of gaining greater clarity, consider the following questions/areas.

TYPES OF TECHNOLOGY

- ☑ What kinds of devices (for example, smartphones, tablets, laptops, desktops, drones, television) are appropriate for your kids given their ages?
- ☑ What types of shows and channels are aligned with your values? Which ones are not?
- ☑ What applications, or apps, are aligned with your family culture? Which ones do not fit?
- ☑ How does social media fit within your family culture/values? What about posting information on social media? What is considered appropriate? What websites are off limits? What web sites are aligned with your values and family culture?
- ☑ Be sure to include this in your family blueprint and expectations for your kids.

MONITORING USE

- ☑ What is your plan for monitoring your kids' technology use?
- ☑ What is your plan for monitoring your use?
- ☑ How will you be reviewing their posts and text messages? Have you explained this to your kids?
- ☑ If you are not sure how to monitor, who can help you learn?
- ☑ What parental controls will you employ on various websites and apps?
- ☑ Be sure to include this in your family blueprint and expectations for your kids.

FREQUENCY OF USE

- ☑ How frequently can your children use technology?
- ☑ How much time per day is allotted for screen time?
- ☑ What time do screens need to be shut down at night?
- ☑ What are the parameters around use? Are they allowed to use technology before school? During school? During homework?
- ☑ During family meals and other family times, what are your expectations for use or nonuse of technology?
- ☑ Be sure to include this in your family blueprint and expectations for your kids.

CHAPTER 10: BOUNDARIES, LIMITS, & CONSEQUENCES WITH TECHNOLOGY

TECHNOLOGY MANAGEMENT

As a values grounded parent, it can be rather helpful to approach the issue of technology from a *management* perspective. In other words, explore how you want to manage your kids' and your screen time so that you remain aligned with your positive values and family culture. It also affords your kids the opportunity to practice self-management in efforts to achieve balance.

A quick note on self-management versus management by others: As a values grounded parent, it is important to consistently monitor your children's behavior to determine how well they can manage on their own and to what degree you need to step in and help them manage. As your children try to learn the skills toward self-management, they will certainly make mistakes.

Let's look at an example. My teenage daughter received a phone as an early 16th birthday present. In our family, we opted to wait until our kids were 16. The thinking was that they would be more mature in managing the device and would have a phone if they were in an emergency while driving.

My daughter received her phone several months early—my wife talked with me about the necessity of our daughter having a phone to communicate regarding her dance schedule and rehearsals (structured flexibility). We both agreed (United Front) that she was mature enough for a phone. We reviewed expectations with her and offered her an opportunity to self-manage. Initially, she showed great self-management skills. There were no issues for a while. Then, we started noticing she was going to bed in the early hours of the morning. It became apparent she was on the device past midnight and struggling with disconnecting.

VALUES GROUNDED PARENTING

We reviewed the value of her getting a good night's rest and disconnecting from the device at least a half hour before she went to bed. She assured us that she understood the boundary and the value (self-care) it was reinforcing. She requested that she have an opportunity to try to self-manage. Since she seemed to understand her mistake, we supported opportunities for her to learn greater balance with technology use.

Things went well for a couple of weeks, and then we noticed that she was staying up late again. So, we stepped in, explaining that she was not being balanced in her ability at managing her phone use with our agreed expectations. We explained that her phone needed to be handed over by 9:30 p.m. on weeknights. Although she did not like it, she did understand it. By approaching technology management this way, we avoided an unnecessary power struggle and used a consequence to help her learn from her mistake.

So, in the spirit of technology management, the following steps are recommended:

STEP 1:

Gain clarity on types of screens, frequency of use, and plan for monitoring use. Clarify these issues with your spouse/partner (United Front) before having a family meeting. It is important for you to be in agreement before approaching this issue with your children.

STEP 2:

Call a family meeting. Since technology is a meaningful activity for most kids, allow extra time for discussion. Review the questions and invite your children to explore how to engage technology in a manner that is aligned with your values and family culture. Remember to take time to listen to your children's perspectives and feelings.

- Step 2a: Develop a plan for monitoring their use. Be very specific and assert your right as a parent to supervise their use—checking text messages, reviewing posts, and so on.
- Step 2b: Clearly identify frequency of use and consequences if the plan is not followed.

STEP 3:

Focus on consistency in your efforts to maintain boundaries and limits around time of use and frequency.

STEP 4:

Develop a *technology management contract* that clearly defines roles and responsibilities in effective management. Also, clearly define negative consequences if the contract is not followed. A sample contract can be found in **Appendix C**. You can search the internet for a variety of other, similar types of contracts.

SUMMARY AND TAKEAWAYS

- A technological revolution is underway. It is a visible and meaningful part of our culture.
    - Technology use is integrated with education, employment, and recreation.
    - Because it is positively reinforcing, most kids and parents struggle with balancing screen time with face-to-face time.
- It is important to develop and support a healthy balance between your family culture and the technological culture.
    - Your shared vision and positive values help you define what a healthy balance is for your kids and family.

- Boundaries, limits, and consequences help reinforce this healthy balance. Clear and consistent boundaries help support face-to-face human connection.
- Approach technology use from a management perspective.
- Develop a plan for how your family will manage technology. Align this plan with your family culture and values.
    - Use Clarity (one of the five C's) in defining clear expectations around technology use.
    - Afford opportunities for your kids to manage their screen use and step in when their behavior indicates that they are mismanaging or being ungrounded in their efforts.
    - Examine your own use of technology and seek a healthy balance. Your children need your attention and emotional presence to help them grow up.
    - Consider use of behavior contracts. Documents like these help redirect kids AND parents from their emotions toward expectations.

CHAPTER 11
DISCIPLINE: STAY GROUNDED OR BE GROUNDED

DISCIPLINE IS A TYPE OF CONSEQUENCE that is designed to help ***ground*** your kids when they behave in ***ungrounded*** ways. This type of consequence serves to reconnect them with the importance of behaving in accordance with their values. The ultimate goal is for your kids to consistently ground their behavior in positive values so they don't need you or others to ground them. Of course, this takes time (for some, a lifetime!), especially as your kids take on the battle of wants versus needs.

When applied effectively, discipline is designed to move your kids out of their comfort zone. The reason for moving your kids out of their comfort zone is twofold: 1) You do not want your kids to get comfortable with the idea of behaving in ungrounded ways, and 2) When your kids are out of their comfort zone, they are in a place where meaningful learning and growth can occur.

The key is to allow them the space to feel the consequences of the discipline and process it in a way that helps them learn that their behavior and decision making need to change.

CHAPTER 11: DISCIPLINE

Let's look at a common example. Let's say a preteen (12-year-old) is playing an online game with his buddies. Before he starts the game, he lies to his parents about completing his homework, telling them that it was all done when in fact it was not. As part of their family blueprint (as outlined in a technology contract), the expectations clearly indicate that homework and other values grounded responsibilities need to be completed *before* any screen use. The child knowingly lies in efforts to do what he wants and avoid what he needs to do (Wants versus Needs).

The child does not realize or simply forgets that most parents, especially moms, have a superpower in sniffing out dishonesty. His mom checks and discovers that his homework was not done. The mom addresses this with her son. Making no eye contact, he continues to play while attempting to tell another lie about his homework.

His mom sets a firm boundary, explaining in behavioral words that he needs to disengage from the computer and go to his room. He protests, emotionally pleading for another five minutes, saying he will then do his homework. His mom leans into the principles of the five C's, and remains consistent, clear, and calm with the limits. His mom explains that if he does not walk to his room, the device will be removed. The son yells at his mom, cursing and slinging insults, telling her that he's going to do whatever he wants and she cannot control him. He then storms to his room.

As you can see, the son's behavior is ungrounded. The values of honesty, accountability, and respect were absent in his decision making and behavior. The mom recognizes that her son will benefit from being grounded. She discusses the need for grounding with her husband (a United Front). Both parents are in agreement that grounding would be beneficial, and they discuss the details of the negative consequences.

VALUES GROUNDED PARENTING

The mom gives her son some time to calm down before addressing the consequences of his ungrounded behavior. After he settles, she then talks with him about his dishonest and disrespectful behavior. She explains that since he did not ground himself in behavior that reflects his values, she will ground him.

The grounding consists of loss of screen and technology privileges for one week and grounding to his room for the weekend (no friends). The idea of losing screen privileges as well as missing out with his friends creates a significant degree of discomfort for him. He does not like the consequences whatsoever.

The son goes to his father and explains that "mom is being totally unfair." He hopes that his father will understand this and allow him to go hang out with his buddy over the weekend. Using a "both/and" approach, the father validates his son's feelings AND redirects him to examine his behavior that led to his grounding. The son feels upset and tells his father he does not understand and care. The father clarifies that understanding and caring do not necessarily mean agreeing with him and his perspective.

Maintaining a United Front, the father explains to his son that he is to complete three writing tasks while he is grounded. First, he is to write three reasons why honesty is important in his relationships and two ways that being honest will help him grow up in a healthy way. Second, he is to write three ways to handle frustrating and angry feelings in respectful ways and two ways that expressing such strong emotion respectfully will help him grow into a healthy young man. Third, he is to write an apology for his disrespectful behavior.

Through this process, the child is afforded the space to experience the emotional consequences and discomfort related to his ungrounded behavior. This space also affords him an opportunity to learn about the

CHAPTER 11: DISCIPLINE

impact of his ungrounded behavior on others. Equally important, he also learns how staying grounded will help him grow, learn, and thrive.

WINDSHIELD THINKING AND EFFECTIVE DISCIPLINE

As reflected in the example above, discipline often elicits strong emotion. It is key to keep your focus on the underlying purpose of the discipline. The value of discipline teaches your kids several important lessons:

1. Their behavior is ungrounded and needs to change.
2. They need to reflect on their decision making that led them to behave in ungrounded ways.
3. Their behavior needs to demonstrate positive values.

Remember the tree-pruning example from Chapter 7. In order for the tree to grow in an upward direction, the landscaper prunes the downward-growing branches. Grounding serves to clip those downward-growing behaviors in your children. In the short term, your kids don't like this type of pruning, especially since they are not getting to do what they want (Wants versus Needs Battle). However, over the long term, they learn to use their windshield thinking and make better decisions that help them grow up rather than down.

Grounding reinforces your boundaries and limits. When your kids choose to continue to test limits, grounding redirects them towards their positive values. From a credibility standpoint, grounding crystalizes your role as leaders in the family. If you set a boundary that your kids blow off and you do not enforce it, you are essentially telling your kids they *only need to listen to you some of the time.* ***As indicated earlier, this "some" can quickly turn into a sum.***

THREATS OF GROUNDING

Threats of grounding often occur when parents feel angry, powerless, worn out, and embarrassed by their kids' behavior. Threatening is an impulsive action, lacking a clear and thoughtful plan. We've all been there at one point. Whether it be in the cereal aisle, a birthday party, a school function ... you name it.

Oftentimes, children wait until you are in the public eye to fling themselves on the ground in a tantrum of epic proportions or yell a defiant "NO!" when reminded it is time to leave.

Despite the frustration and stress that comes along with their limit-testing behavior, it is key to practice mindfulness and avoid the temptation to threaten grounding. You may want to let your kids see the depth of irritation their behavior causes, but it is important that you practice patience and mindfulness. When you are calm, you are in a better place to redirect and guide them in handling difficult and snarky emotions.

Just the notion of threatening runs opposite to values grounded parenting. Threats do not belong in a positive family culture.

> **Use limits and consequences to repel and extinguish threats to your family culture and positive values. Do not threaten discipline, especially since discipline is designed to be a positive form of teaching and learning.**

So, rather than threaten, offer a *forecast* for your kids. A forecast, similar to what a weatherman uses, predicts what will happen if the conditions or circumstances continue.

For example, a parent may say to their child (who is refusing to get off their device to do their homework): *"Remember, you are to start your homework in five minutes. If you choose to do so, you get to keep the privilege of using your device. If you don't, you are choosing to lose the privilege. Know that either way, there will be a consequence."*

Notice that the parent completely makes no mention of themselves in the above statement. By leaving their ego out of it, the focus is centered on the child's decision making, behavior, and consequences.

The calmer and less threatening you are, the greater impact discipline and consequences have in shaping and teaching your kids. Let's take a look at different disciplinary approaches.

FOUR TYPES OF DISCIPLINARY APPROACHES

There are different types of disciplinary approaches, four of which are summarized below.

1. *Permissive Parenting*—tendency toward being overly lenient and not following through with consequences. Permissive parents have rules, though they do not consistently reinforce the rules/behavior expectations and are more likely to bend the rules at the protest of their children.

2. *Authoritarian Parenting*—tendency toward being overly strict and rigid, with a "my way or the highway" approach. Authoritarian parents have rules and enforce them with little regard for the child's perspective and emotion. They are more likely to be punitive in their discipline, focusing on control with little opportunity for the child to problem solve and understand the reason for discipline.

3. *Uninvolved Parenting*—tendency to be emotionally and socially disconnected from their kids, not knowing what their kids are doing, or frankly, interested in knowing. The uninvolved parent does not have clearly defined rules or expectations. In fact, this type of parent expects their children to raise themselves. These parents often neglect the needs of helping their kids grow up.

4. *Authoritative Parenting*—tendency to be actively involved in the child's life, rules are clearly defined and consistently enforced, and positive reinforcement is frequently used. These parents tend to involve their children in problem solving and help them understand the reason for their discipline.

Which of the four approaches describes your style of discipline? The following activity helps increase mindfulness and awareness about your approach to discipline.

ACTIVITY: SELF REFLECTION ON DISCIPLINE

- Which approach describes the style that you experienced as a child?
- What are the challenges you experience in disciplining your child(ren)?
- What emotions do you experience when disciplining your child?
- How well do you manage these emotions?

CHAPTER 11: DISCIPLINE

ADOPTING THE AUTHORITATIVE PARENTING APPROACH

Which of the four approaches best fits with values grounded parenting? If your answer is Authoritative parenting, you are spot on! Authoritative parenting is associated with confident children, who are more likely to experience long-lasting happiness and success, and better able to make healthy decisions as adults. Permissive parents tend to have children who struggle with rules, expectations, and authority. They tend to be indecisive and experience behavioral problems. Uninvolved parents tend to have children with low self-esteem, experience long-standing sadness/depression, experience behavior problems, and have difficulty with school. Authoritarian parents tend to have children who tend to be rule followers, avoid responsibility for fear of punishment, minimize the value of their opinion and perspective (or the other extreme—overvalue their opinion), and have difficulty with perspective-taking.

So, as you can see, approaching parenting from an authoritative style tends to work best in raising confident, balanced, and joyful children who comprehend the importance of making values grounded decisions.

As you read this, it certainly makes a whole lot of sense, right? So, why can it be so darn challenging to discipline your kids? You may know better, yet find yourself disciplining in a way that runs counter to what you should do. A few of the reasons are described below:

1. Emotion
2. Time
3. Family Blueprint
4. Consistency

VALUES GROUNDED PARENTING

EMOTION

"Why is it that you ALWAYS have to have the last word?!"

"How DARE you say that to me!"

"We JUST talked about this and you did it again!"

"Were you expecting the kitchen fairy to unload the dishwasher?"

"Did you just hit your brother? How would you like it if I hit you in the head?!"

Add your own to the above list. Your emotion can get in the way of disciplining effectively. When your kids test limits, you can find yourself feeling angry, disappointed, frustrated, and worried. You may feel angry at their willful defiance. You may feel let down, disappointed, and frustrated at their lack of desire to motivate and do their work. You may feel hurt by their selfish behavior. Whatever the situation, most loving and caring parents are emotionally triggered by their kids' ungrounded behavior.

What do you think happens to your ability to effectively discipline when you are triggered? Well, if you are like most of us, your stress buttons can blind you from your vision and values. You can easily find yourself parenting out of reactive emotion. For example, you may *yell* at your kids to "STOP YELLING!" You may back talk your 13-year-old who just back talked you! When your three-year-old is throwing a volcanic tantrum, you may have a tantrum of your own.

As discussed earlier, a key part to growing up is developing an emotional vocabulary. As leaders of your family, you set the tone by modeling how to manage and express emotion in healthy, values grounded ways. On certain days, this task is easier said than done. However, practicing emotional awareness and managing your stress buttons will help reduce overreactions (yelling, hollering, and threatening) to your kids' misbehavior.

Here are some warning signs that you are emotionally triggered:

- ⇨ Power struggles with your kids
- ⇨ Yelling and screaming at your kids
- ⇨ Verbal threats of punishment
- ⇨ Shutting down and disengaging from your kids

A NOTE ABOUT ANGER

Anger is often a camouflaged emotion—it camouflages other feelings underlying or fueling the anger. For example, if you feel ignored by your kids, you may feel angry, but underlying the anger can be feelings of dismissiveness, rejection, and hurt. You may feel angry at your kids for making the same mistake again and again, though underlying the anger can be feelings of concern and helplessness.

So, why does anger camouflage more vulnerable feelings? Anger can be a safer emotion to express. Both children and parents may hide behind their anger as a way to avoid their vulnerability. Additionally, many parents and kids struggle with finding the right words to express their strong emotion, leading to avoidance and bottling their feelings. Of course, when emotion is bottled up, it builds up pressure and the release can be an angry tirade.

Anger can also yield power. The angrier you get, the stronger and tougher you may feel. You may use anger as a way of setting a boundary to let others know you are not playing around or to back off. Expressions of anger, like a loud and intimidating voice, serve to get attention and may be used to get others to comply with your requests. This happens a lot in the case of a parent-child power struggle. Both child and parent escalate in their efforts to assert their power.

VALUES GROUNDED PARENTING

One way to disengage from power struggles is to set an emotional boundary so you do not personalize the stress of your child's ungrounded behavior. *Allow them the opportunity to face the emotional consequences of their actions by staying firm, calm, and focused in your discipline.* Use the "both/and" approach, where you can validate your child's emotion and redirect their negative behavior. When your kids see that you will not be emotionally unhinged by their behavior and the discipline is clear and consistent, they begin to have a meaningful experience of the consequences for their actions.

Here are some tips to manage emotional stress and avoid being triggered:

- ☑ On your way home from work, play some soothing and relaxing music to help you de-stress from the day or play some comedy stations to help lighten the mood.

- ☑ Engage in 4-7-8 breathing before addressing a disciplinary situation with your child (this technique is reviewed in the Mindfulness section in Chapter 4).

- ☑ Remember that testing limits and discipline are part of all children's path toward growing up. Children do not grow up without making mistakes and testing limits. Anticipate this as part of raising children.

- ☑ Develop a script or phrase to use with your kids when triggered. For example, "I am very upset right now and need to take a cool-down. We will talk later."

CHAPTER 11: DISCIPLINE

TIME

How many of you feel rushed and constantly on the go? Do you find yourself trying to squeeze yet one more activity in an already packed day or week? It is a sign of the times, racing around to drop off and pick up your kids, fit a store run in, prep meals, and field emails and calls from work.

Carving out quality time with your children is essential for discipline to work effectively. By consistently spending quality time with your kids, you grow love, intimacy, and value in your relationships. This ensures that you don't just give them your attention when they need discipline. In order to grow **value**, you have to **spend**! *Time is one of the most precious gifts of all.* Spending time sends the message that your children are loved and valued. Remember, you don't get this time back—make the best use of it while you have it.

On the other hand, if you neglect spending time with your kids, their sense of value can diminish. In my clinical practice, it is common to see kids act out as a way of drawing a parent back into their lives. Even though the child's ungrounded behavior may invite negative attention, it is still emotional attention. Be on the lookout for this and make time to spend with your kids.

Here are some suggestions:

- ☑ Meet your kids at school for lunch (once a month). If your kids are in elementary school, meet them in the school cafeteria and bring along a treat. This not only makes your child feel special, but it also allows you to meet some of their friends. When your child talks about their day at school, you will know many of their friends. I also recommend going out to the recess yard after lunch to play with your child and their friends. Don't worry about getting your work clothes dirty—the joy it

brings you and your child is well worth it!
- ☑ Take a ten-minute walk together around the neighborhood a few times a week.
- ☑ Have regular/monthly family meetings. Go over your family blueprint, positive values, and feedback. Make popcorn or another yummy treat to make the meetings a bit more fun and engaging.
- ☑ Wrestle and goof around. Play with your kids. For children, play is their language and a huge part of their growing and learning. Being part of this enables you to learn and grow with them.
- ☑ After disciplining your child, follow up with them to let them know it is NOT personal. **Remind them that your love for them goes well beyond their mistakes.**
- ☑ Before the grounding is over, review with them what they learned from their mistake and how will they do things differently next time.
- ☑ Block time out in your schedule to ensure that rules and expectations are followed.
  - ✓ Be on hand to ensure that the bedtime routine is followed. Avoid the temptation to retreat to the screen or your room.
  - ✓ Check your kids' chores to ensure they were completed and done with care.
  - ✓ Be on hand to ensure that homework is completed. If you are at work, a quick phone call lets your child know you are *invested* in the *value* in their learning.

CHAPTER 11: DISCIPLINE

FAMILY BLUEPRINT

In the chapter on family culture, your family blueprint was discussed—hopefully, you completed the activity and developed/refined your blueprint. One of the key subject areas was discipline. Let's briefly revisit this as it carries the importance of a second mention.

How does your family of origin blueprint influence the way you currently discipline your kids? First and foremost, it is helpful to assess if the discipline methods you experienced as a child were values grounded and effective.

Some of you may have had experiences where your ***authoritative*** parents applied consistent and firm natural and logical consequences. You learned from your consequences and trusted your parents to guide you. Discipline was focused on your misbehavior/mistake and how you could learn from it. When disciplined, you felt guilty for your behavior and understood that you were a good kid whose behavior was bad.

Some of you endured experiences where your ***authoritarian*** parents were harsh and punitive. You learned to fear consequences and avoid discipline as it was a hurtful and scary experience. When being disciplined, you felt ashamed as your parents saw your behavior as a reflection of you being a bad kid as opposed to a good kid who behaved badly.

Some of you had experiences where your ***permissive*** parents were overly lenient and inconsistent with their discipline. You learned that consequences were merely words, mostly because your parents were upset at the time. Once they calmed down, the consequence would be reduced or just not enforced. You may have learned that if you protested and debated their discipline, your efforts would lead to getting out of the consequence or having it significantly reduced. You felt you were a good kid and your parents were not good at disciplining you.

Some of you had experiences where your ***uninvolved*** parents were absent when it came time for discipline. You learned that it was up to you to discipline yourself. You learned that you could do what you wanted and often had to face discipline outside the home. You learned that discipline was a way to avoid trouble as opposed to an opportunity to learn and grow. If you did learn and grow from it, it typically was the result of a coach, teacher, and/or good friend. When being disciplined, you may have felt upset because of the inconvenience of the consequences.

The power and influence of your family of origin blueprint is strong. How many of you have ever said, "My goodness, I sound just like my mom" or "I am turning into my dad!" For most, there are positives and negatives of disciplining like your parents. *Your goal is to dilute the dysfunction and grow the positives.*

The following activity will help you gain greater clarity on the negatives and positives that come from your family blueprint.

CONSISTENCY

Similar to the family blueprint, consistency warrants a second mention on account of its importance. As you may recall, consistency is interchangeable with trust. When you are consistent with values grounded discipline, your kids trust that you are committed to helping them grow, learn, and thrive—even though they don't like the experience of being grounded.

With that said, a common mistake parents make is being inconsistent with boundaries and discipline. As stated earlier, your own emotion and family blueprint can contribute to your inconsistency. Some parents present a tough talk when it comes to delivering firm and consistent discipline, yet buckle and soften when it is time to follow through. Children study your every move, and they know if you have a tendency to buckle. The bottom line is your kids lose trust in you and in your shared vision if you remain indecisive and inconsistent with discipline.

ACTIVITY: DISCIPLINARY STYLES FROM OUR FAMILY BLUEPRINT

- Growing up, which of the disciplinary methods (Authoritarian, Authoritative, Permissive, Uninvolved) fit your parents' approach with you?

- When being disciplined, did you feel that you were a bad kid or your behavior was bad?

- What did you learn from your parents' discipline? Did you feel like your parents were using discipline to teach consequences or more as harsh punishment?

- How has your parents' discipline approach influenced the way you currently discipline?

- Identify at least one change you can make to use discipline as a means to help your kids grow and learn (for example, being more consistent with follow-through or, when grounding your child, asking them to write a paragraph on what they learned from their mistake and how this will help them be more values grounded).

VALUES GROUNDED PARENTING

I remember a family I worked with awhile back. The parents and I spent part of our session discussing appropriate discipline for their seven-year-old son who punched a friend after he snatched one of his prized superhero action figures. This seven-year-old reacted impulsively to his anger—sort of a ready, fire, aim approach. He understood what he did was wrong. The parents discussed his grounding to be twofold: 1) He was to apologize to his friend and do something nice for him, and 2) he would be grounded to the house for the weekend as a reminder that he needs to practice sharing and show self-control when upset.

After hearing about his grounding, the boy became very sad, in a sort of panicked way. He tearfully pleaded with his parents to not ground him because he and his buddy were making plans for a campout sleepover in his backyard. His cries escalated, apologizing profusely. The parents proceeded to say, *"Well, we'll talk about this when we get home."* The boy's mood improved rather quickly. I strongly encouraged the parents to remain consistent and firm. The boy sheepishly asked his parents if they could get ice cream on the way home from my office. The parents reluctantly agreed. Well, take a guess on whether the parents remained consistent with their grounding.

When the parents returned to their next session, they had a defeated expression. They explained that they did not ground their son and allowed him to have a campout with his friend. They proceeded to say that the campout was cut short because both boys got into an argument, and their son reportedly called his friend some horrible names and pushed him. The reason for the argument: their son would not share his toys. The parents were astonished, thinking that removing the grounding would help him be a more generous, cooperative friend. As this example illustrates, consistency and follow-through are key to helping your kids learn from the process of being grounded.

CHAPTER 11: DISCIPLINE

EFFECTIVE DISCIPLINE: CONTROLLING YOUR BEHAVIOR AND HOME ENVIRONMENT

Have you ever tried to stop your child from whining? Fussing? Make them change their snarky tone?

How about trying to make them eat a certain food? Wear clothing that you favor?

What impact does trying to control your child's behavior have on your relationship with them?

The Golden Rule in disciplining your kids: *You are far more effective when you focus your thoughts and actions on the things you can control, like your behavior and home environment, and NOT trying to control your kids' behavior.*

A key move in practicing effective discipline is liberating yourself from the belief that you HAVE to MAKE your children listen and behave. Buying into this belief will send you down a path of much frustration, anger, and helplessness, fueling unproductive power struggles. Furthermore, the positive intimacy in your relationship with your kids will be drained, and they will see your efforts as anything but values grounded.

So, does this mean you let your kids run amuck? Of course not. As stated earlier, disciplining children is crucial in helping them grow up in a healthy way. As values grounded parents, focus your efforts on things you have control over, like your behavior and home environment. By so doing, you control things like your volume, tone, and actions so that they are calm, firm, and consistent. Model the behavior you want to see your kids demonstrate.

Practicing values grounded parenting means handling your kids' disrespectful and irresponsible behavior in respectful and responsible ways. Focus your efforts on practicing the five C's (consistency, competency, clarity, calmness, and consequences). Consistently practice the VPC approach (Validate, Promote, and Consequence) and allow consequences to teach and instruct your kids.

In efforts to control your home environments, take steps like removing toys out of your kids' room while they are grounded. This affords them the space and quiet time to reflect on their decision making and behavior. Remove electronic devices to ensure they are free from distractions while being grounded. It also affords them the time to complete any worksheets and writing assignments that you assign.

WRITING ASSIGNMENTS

The use of writing assignments makes the discipline process more productive by inviting self-reflection. A key developmental task is for kids to develop a capacity to self monitor—this means to think about how their behavior affects others, themselves, and future outcomes. By assigning writing tasks, you can invite your child to think about their decision making and ungrounded behavior. When giving writing assignments, consider the following recommendations:

- ☑ Make the assignment consistent with your child's age and grade level.
    - ✓ With children who have yet to learn to write, consider asking them to draw a picture or draw a picture together of what happened. Ask them how they felt, how others felt and help them draw it. Ask them what they could do differently next time and how it would make them and others feel.
    - ✓ With children who are learning to write, ask them what was wrong about their behavior and what they could do differently. Next, print their responses and ask them to practice their writing by copying the printed responses.
- ☑ Include your positive values in the assignment. Ask your child

to write a paragraph/several sentences linking their decision making and behavior to their positive values.
- ☑ Request they write two or three ways they can practice or behave according to their values.
- ☑ Include your vision in the assignment. Ask your child to explain how behaving in keeping with their values will help them grow up.
- ☑ Consider using a "Mistake Made and Lesson Learned" Worksheet. In *Appendix D*, there are some samples for you to use.
- ☑ Be sure to ask your child to write an apology for their behavior.

The effectiveness of the writing assignment is related to your taking time to review it. Be sure to process their written response and lessons learned.

DISCIPLINING YOUR KIDS: A STEPWISE APPROACH

Let's pull it all together and look at some concrete steps to take when disciplining your kids:

STEP 1: Clarify with your co-parent the need for discipline and review the details; for example, the reason for being grounded and the length and parameters of the grounding. This helps you maintain a United Front so that your kids don't play one parent against the other. Clarify the value(s) you want to teach your child through the disciplinary process.

STEP 2: Have a talk with your child and identify and label their ungrounded behavior. Examples:

"Your behavior was dishonest."

"Your behavior was irresponsible."

"Your behavior was disruptive and lacks self-control."

Be sure to separate the person from the behavior. Examples:

"Your behavior was dishonest" versus *"You are a liar!"*

"Your behavior was irresponsible" versus *"You are a slacker/lazy!"*

"Your behavior was disrespectful" versus *"You are rude and selfish."*

"Your behavior was disruptive and lacks self-control" versus *"You can't lose it like that. You embarrassed me in the store."*

STEP 3: Link their ungrounded behavior to a value(s). Examples:

"When you cheated (ungrounded behavior) on the test, your actions showed a lack of honesty (value)."

"When you avoided your homework by playing video games (ungrounded behavior), your actions showed a lack of responsibility (value)."

"When you use bad/negative/curse words (ungrounded behavior), your actions show a lack of respect (value)."

"When you yell and throw a tantrum (ungrounded behavior), your actions show a lack of self-control (value)."

As evident in the above examples, the focus is on the child's behavior and values. The parent removes their ego from the disciplinary process.

CHAPTER 11: DISCIPLINE

STEP 4: Link how the value is an important part of their process of growing up in a healthy way *(shared vision)*. Examples:

"As you know, honesty is an important value that builds and maintains trust in your relationships. Consistently practicing honesty is an important part of growing up in a healthy way."

"As you know, responsibility is an important value that helps you be a solid and productive worker. Consistently practicing responsibility is an important part of growing up in a healthy way."

"As you are learning, respect is an important value that strengthens your relationships. Using respectful words, especially when you're upset, is an important part of growing up."

"As you are learning, self-control is an important value that helps you deal with anger in good ways. Consistently practicing self-control is an important part of growing up."

STEP 5: Clarify the need for their behavior to change and the use of a consequence to facilitate meaningful change. Examples:

"Your behavior needs to change and reflect greater honesty. To help you see this, you will be grounded for the weekend. This means you are grounded from electronics and friends. Additionally, you are to complete (writing assignment, tailored for their age), identifying the importance of honesty and how it helps you grow up."

"Your behavior needs to change and reflect greater responsibility. I understand the temptation to avoid homework, though please know that we do not support avoidance in our family. To help you understand this, you are grounded from electronics/video games for the next three days."

"Your behavior needs to change and show greater respect. I understand it is hard to express frustrating feelings in respectful ways. However, just because it is hard does not mean it is impossible and that you get a pass. Rather, part of growing up means stepping in to do tough things, as this makes you tougher and better able to handle stressful situations respectfully. To help you better understand this, you are grounded for the evening. This means no electronics, no playing in your room. Additionally, you are to complete (writing assignment, tailored for their age), identifying the value in using respectful words to express frustrating and stressful feelings."

*"Your behavior needs to change and show greater self-control. I understand you were very upset and it can be difficult to be so upset **and** be in control of your behavior at the same time. But, just because it is hard to do, does not mean it is impossible or that you should not try or practice. It is important to maintain self-control in the face of angry, frustrating, and stressful feelings. By so doing, you build self-confidence in dealing with tough feelings and circumstances. To help you understand this better, you are being grounded to your room with no electronics, play, or time with friends for the remainder of the day. Additionally, you are to complete (writing assignment, tailored for their age), identifying the value of being in control of your behavior while being upset at the same time."*

CHAPTER 11: DISCIPLINE

STEP 6: Remain consistent with follow-through and do not buckle or water down the consequences because your child is uncomfortable with the experience of being grounded.

Remember: The discipline process is designed to teach kids that their behavior is ungrounded. If they are out of their comfort zone, that is okay. Some of our greatest learning and life lessons often occur when we are out of our comfort zone.

DISCIPLINE AND EMOTION

As discussed earlier, your emotional triggers can interfere with and mess up your efforts toward effective discipline. Whether it be your emotion, the emotion of your child, or both, be mindful and humble in using this awareness to your advantage.

It is recommended that you levy the consequence *after* both your and your child's emotion is settled. If you discipline when you are very upset, you are more likely to overreact in a harsh and punitive way. You may find yourself grounding your kids until they are 30 years old! If you try to levy the negative consequences when you child is very upset, they are less likely to hear you and the positive purpose underlying the discipline.

So, what do you do when it is time to deliver consequences and emotion is running at distressingly high levels? Take a moment to set an emotional boundary and allow some time for things to calm down. In some instances, it may take just a few minutes, and in other instances, it may take a few hours. However long the time, it is good practice to apply consequences when you and your kids are calm.

So, what does it look like when you set a boundary to help calm the emotion? You engage the Validate, Promote, and Consequence (VPC) approach. As a brief reminder, you validate your child's emotion/experience, promote the desired behavior, and provide a consequence.

Here are some examples:

"I see that you are very upset, and what you have to say is important. Right now, you are too upset and your voice is too loud for us to have a good conversation. Please go to your room, calm down, and we will discuss this after you are calmer."

"I see that you are angry and upset. We do need to talk about this. It is hard to listen and have a good talk when you are so angry. Please go to your room, calm yourself—remember you can do some breathing—and we will discuss consequences later."

"Right now I am too upset to discuss your behavior. Please go to your room. I need some time to settle myself. We will discuss this later."

Of course, once the emotion has settled, you are much better able to engage your rational mind. When engaging your rational mind, you are more likely to apply consequences that are reasonable and support your values grounded efforts. Similarly, your kids are better able to re-engage their rational minds. They are more likely to separate their behavior from their person and understand the purpose for the consequences.

DEBRIEFING AND DISCUSSING THE DISCIPLINE

A key part of the discipline process with your children involves having meaningful conversations regarding the disciplinary incident and related consequence. These kinds of conversations serve as a fertilizer for learning and growth. By debriefing and discussing the incident, you get to hear your kids' perspective. You can both share feedback that helps you grow from the experience.

Furthermore, conversations about discipline provide you with a key opportunity to clarify the purpose of the negative consequence(s).

CHAPTER 11: DISCIPLINE

One way to accomplish this is to use the strategy of linking—link your child's behavior with the negative consequence and positive values.

In efforts to support a positive family culture, emphasize with your kids that discussing mistakes, ungrounded behavior, and discipline is part of how you work together as a family. This way, you are establishing that these conversations, as uncomfortable as they might be, are key to learning and growing.

DIALOGUE NOT MONOLOGUE

When discussing the discipline, it is important to have a dialogue and not a monologue. It is good practice to avoid making the discipline process lecture driven. If your kids are like most, they will tune you out like a bad radio station. When I was a director of a private school, I learned that effective teachers speak less than 50 percent of class time. Since discipline is designed to teach, it is important to invite your kids to participate and avoid "punishment by lecture."

One way of promoting participation is to be curious and ask open-ended questions. Below are some questions to consider when discussing discipline, ungrounded behavior, and values. Many of the questions imply that your kids have a decent command of language. The younger the child, the more "Dr. Seuss–like" your conversation ought to be. Keeping your conversation simple and brief helps them see that their behavior is a problem and needs to change.

Here are some questions that help open up space for discipline conversations:

- ⇨ What did you do (that led to your grounding)? How did you get in trouble? (Let's keep in mind that behavior that is ungrounded is indeed . . . troubling!)
- ⇨ What was the reason you did it (what was your intent/purpose

behind the behavior)?
- ⇨ From your eyes/perspective, what makes your behavior problematic?
- ⇨ What could you do differently next time? (Know better, do better.)
- ⇨ Can you see that your behavior was ungrounded? What value or values were missing?

- ⇨ What can you learn from this situation that will help you in the future?
- ⇨ What can you do to ground yourself in how you behave these values so you don't need to be grounded for this again?
- ⇨ If you do not improve in practicing your values, what impact will this have on your life at home/school /with friends? (This is a good topic to ask your child to write about.)

Let's remember that it is not easy to consistently behave in values grounded ways. It takes a great deal of self-discipline, requiring prudence and ongoing practice. Anticipate that your kids will make mistakes and be ready to use discipline to provide corrective feedback. Discipline will redirect them toward growing up as opposed to growing down.

The process of correcting ungrounded behavior often creates conflict. As we will see in the next chapter, conflict is a catalyst for growth and learning.

CHAPTER 11: DISCIPLINE

SUMMARY AND TAKEAWAYS

- Discipline has a positive purpose despite the use of a negative consequence. It serves to prune downward-growing behaviors.
- Threats of discipline or grounding are ineffective. Use forecasting instead of threats.
    - Forecast the consequences of what will happen as opposed to making reactive threats.
    - Threats undermine your family culture.
- There are four general types of parenting approaches:
    - Authoritative
    - Authoritarian
    - Permissive
    - Uninvolved
    - Authoritative parenting and values grounded approaches use a similar disciplinary style
- Keys to effective discipline:
    - Stay focused on your shared vision and the purpose for the discipline.
    - Take your ego out of it.
    - Spend quality time with your kids, as this grows love, intimacy, and value.
    - Spend time following through with your discipline.
    - Be consistent, aligning your actions with your words.
    - Understand how you were disciplined as a child and how this influences your disciplinary approach today. Keep the positives and change the negatives.
- Link discipline with your child's behavior and values.
- Present a United Front with your spouse/co-parent when disciplining.

- Use self-discipline when disciplining.
  - Stay calm and focused on the purpose of discipline to avoid overreactions.
  - Avoid disciplining when very upset. Take a cool-down and practice mindfulness so you are modeling the self-discipline you are asking your kids to practice.
- As part of the discipline process, debrief with your kids.
  - Have a conversation (dialogue, not a monologue) about their mistake.
  - Ask open-ended questions.
  - Remind your children that your love for them is much bigger than their mistakes.

PILLAR IV
PRODUCTIVE CONFLICT, MISTAKES, & GROWTH OPPORTUNITIES

CHAPTER 12

PRODUCTIVE CONFLICT AS A CATALYST FOR GROWTH

IT IS LATE ON A THURSDAY AFTERNOON. Mr. Jones turns on the family computer and clicks on the internet. He checks the history and discovers several pornographic websites were viewed in the last couple of days. David, his preteen son, was using the computer during this time. His breath is taken away. *Oh, man, he is only 12 years old*, he thinks to himself.

Mr. Jones knows something needs to be said and done, though it is an awkward and uncomfortable topic to talk about. In maintaining a United Front, he discusses the issue with his wife. They develop a plan of action together. Given the nature of the issue and topic, it is deemed best for Mr. Jones to have a conversation with David.

Although feeling disappointed, upset, and concerned, Mr. Jones does not want the focus of their conversation to be on him and his emotions. He does not want to provoke a destructive conflict with his son. So, he takes a few moments to ensure he is calm (five C's), and meets with his son to have a private, yet meaningful, conversation.

He finds a quiet room and sits down face to face with David to address the conflict around healthy sexuality. After explaining what he

CHAPTER 12: PRODUCTIVE CONFLICT AS A CATALYST FOR GROWTH

discovered on the computer, David gulps nervously, looks toward the ground, and nods to confirm that it was him who searched those sites. Mr. Jones can tell that his son feels ashamed by his actions as well as vulnerable in addressing this conflict. He praises his son's honesty and courage in facing this uncomfortable topic.

The father inquires if David sees his behavior as inappropriate or ungrounded. Again, David nods. In efforts to involve his son more, Mr. Jones asks David what was inappropriate or ungrounded about his behavior. David explains that the images and videos show sex in a bad way. Mr. Jones agrees, and further inquires what his son meant by "bad." David shrugs his shoulders and remains quiet.

Mr. Jones asks his son about the experience of viewing the sexually explicit images and videos. In particular, he asks David if he felt torn—part of him liking it and part of him feeling it was naughty and wrong. David nods, and his eyes well up with tears. His father validates his son's feelings, noting that sexuality often brings up conflicting emotion.

Continuing to take the lead in the conversation, his father explains that David's curiosities and interest in sex are a natural and normal part of growing up from a boy to a man. Leaning into the value of humility, Mr. Jones also explains that dealing with sexual curiosities, thoughts, and feelings is tough, confusing, and not easy for a lot of guys, both boys AND adult men. He notes that a good number of guys struggle with various conflicts around healthy sexuality.

His father goes on to say, *"Just because it is awkward and stressful to deal with does not mean it is unhealthy or wrong to face it and talk about."* In fact, he explains that opening up conversation around healthy sexuality helps reduce stress and confusion as well as clarify appropriate versus inappropriate ways of managing one's sexuality.

VALUES GROUNDED PARENTING

Continuing to practice humility, Mr. Jones goes on to say that he had his share of challenges, questions, and curiosities about healthy sexuality when he was David's age. David now is making eye contact with this father, no longer looking toward the ground in a shame-based way. The conflict and challenge of dealing with his emerging sexuality is seeming less threatening and anxiety provoking and more inviting.

Mr. Jones explains that an important part of growing into a values grounded young man involves developing a healthy concept of (way of dealing with) sexuality. He notes that this conversation is one step toward that goal. Healthy sexuality involves understanding the purpose of sex and the beautiful intimacy that accompanies it.

Given the value of talking about healthy sexuality in supporting David's emerging manhood, they both agree to discuss this topic on a regular basis. They make a father-son pledge to not let the stress or awkwardness keep them from talking about this important subject. The next step is to discuss the basic facts around sex. They agree to meet the following week.

The father also clarifies an expectation for David to manage his sexuality in healthy ways by practicing self-control in the face of temptation to search inappropriate websites. They both agree that it would be good to use adult controls and firewalls as an added boundary.

The example above reflects a process known as *productive conflict*. In a matter of a ten-minute values grounded conversation, the father and son engage the difficult and emotionally conflicted topic of sexuality in a productive manner, leading to continued learning and growth opportunities (an agreement for future conversations and discussions). By engaging the value of humility, the father helped normalize his son's experience as well as shrink the shame around this hard-to-approach, and often, secret subject.

CHAPTER 12: PRODUCTIVE CONFLICT AS A CATALYST FOR GROWTH

Within the values grounded framework, conflict is viewed as a part of any healthy relationship. Even though conflict can move you out of your comfort zone, it serves as a valuable tool to learn and grow. The key is managing it in a productive or constructive way.

In the sections that follow, we will examine conflict from a developmental learning perspective and identify some different approaches—both healthy and unhealthy. Next, productive and destructive conflict will be defined followed by real world examples. You will have an opportunity to see what both types of conflict look and sound like.

Productive conflict is a key part within the values grounded framework. As you will see in this chapter and the next, learning how to engage and manage conflict productively will not only help you establish more balanced relationships with your children, but protect your family culture as well.

CONFLICT PROMOTES GROWTH

Conflict is an important part of your learning process. When managed productively, it serves as a catalyst for advancement and growth. As some of you read the above statement, you may be thinking, *Heck, I bought this book because we have too much conflict at home. How can conflict be helpful for learning when it seems to be wreaking havoc in my relationships with my kids? Isn't conflict a sign of dysfunction in relationships? Shouldn't healthy and values grounded relationships be free from conflict?* If any of those statements capture your thoughts, I understand, especially since I had similar ones years ago.

So, how do conflict and learning go together? Simply put, conflict moves you out of your comfort zone. By being out of your comfort zone, you find yourself in an unfamiliar place where you can experience life from a different perspective(s). From that different perspective comes new knowledge, advancement in your understanding, and wonderful growth possibilities. *Conflict is often essential for meaningful growth as most parents and children don't readily place themselves in uncomfortable places that afford a different view of their world.*

The fact that conflict is a catalyst for learning and growth is by no means a new discovery. Research on learning and cognitive development identified this connection over 80 years ago (Piaget, 1936). Conflict comes from integrating the unfamiliar (new knowledge/experience) with the familiar (old knowledge/experience). In order for you to learn, it is important to accept feedback and new knowledge that you may not have anticipated or expected. This process can involve **growing pains**. As a seasoned dad, I have experienced it and still experience it. As an experienced family therapist, I have had the privilege of helping many clients use conflict to learn, grow, and advance as parents.

As eluded to earlier, the growing up process occurs not just with your kids, but also with you. Think for a moment how you have learned and grown since your kids were born. Challenges and conflict have likely been a meaningful part of your learning. After all, parenting involves on-the-job problem solving as challenges and difficulties surface.

The process of growing up, for both kids AND parents, involves establishing greater comfort with your discomfort.

For many parents and families, exploring their experience and approach to conflict is new territory. Many of you may not think about conflict and how it ought to be managed, let alone be grateful for it. However, let me invite you to take a few steps forward and explore it.

Let's begin this process by examining a couple of common, though dysfunctional, approaches to conflict. The first is "walking on eggshells"

CHAPTER 12: PRODUCTIVE CONFLICT AS A CATALYST FOR GROWTH

or the conflict avoidant approach, and the other is "the bull in a China store." We will then discuss a healthier, more functional approach, "the manager."

WALKING ON EGGSHELLS

When attempting to address conflict, do you feel like you are walking on eggshells? When it comes time to engage in conflict, do you find yourself sidestepping the matter, avoiding direct conversation about the issue? The notion of a person walking on eggshells evokes an image of a need to be *very* careful and cautious about where one is walking. As you can imagine, this approach can be anxiety provoking as well as exhausting.

When one walks on eggshells, they often absorb the emotional tension of the conflicted situation. Conflict avoidance is often fueled by fear. As a result, conflict avoiders expend a great deal of energy trying to control the mood of the situation to temper this fear. They often intercept others who attempt to raise issues in efforts to not cause stress and keep things smooth. This pattern can lead to someone developing control issues in their intimate relationships, fueled by a false sense of control or power—the conflict, *not* the conflict avoider, yields the power.

Conflict avoidance can create a family culture of fragility. Children learn that emotions related to conflict should not be expressed directly for fear of upsetting others. As a result, kids are more likely to internalize their feelings, which can lead to devaluing their emotions and emotional needs (they may see their feelings as bad or wrong). When faced with angry and hurt feelings, they may express their feelings in passive aggressive ways. As they grow up, they are more likely to have lopsided relationships where positive intimacy is stunted when conflict occurs. They miss out on the opportunity to see how engaging in productive conflict can actually strengthen intimacy and trust.

THE BULL IN A CHINA STORE

The opposite approach to walking on eggshells is the bull in the China store. The notion of a bull running through a store with fine China evokes an image of recklessness and destruction. When this perspective is applied to conflict management, a person attempts to dominate conflict through a reactive, haphazard, and oftentimes scary approach. The bull becomes a bully, and this person attempts to use their perceived power to control the conflict through a posture of domination and control.

Behaviors like yelling and threatening are characteristic of this approach. The bull typically does not comprehend the impact their behavior has on others, making it more about them and their degree of stress regarding the conflict. Underlying the yelling and threatening is a need for control. This approach is often consistent with **authoritarian parenting**—one of the four styles discussed in the chapter on discipline.

When conflict is dominated in families, it creates a culture where conflict is scary and unsafe. Children learn that emotion related to conflict is loud, reckless, and hurtful. As a result, they see that conflict is a process of domination and submission. As they grow up, they may identify more with the role of dominating or being submissive. In either role, conflict creates emotional distance and toxic intimacy within their relationships.

WHEN THE CONFLICT STYLES MIX AND MATCH

These two dysfunctional approaches can and often do interact, leading to unhealthy dynamics and relationship patterns. The end result is fractures in trust and positive intimacy, impairing one's ability to pursue their shared vision in helping their children and families learn, grow, and thrive.

For instance, a common dynamic often occurs where the bull in the China store leads to others walking on eggshells. On one hand, you have a family member who is emotionally volatile and others who tend to be emotionally restricted. Underlying this dynamic are misguided efforts to manage or deal with the discomfort that often comes along with conflict.

This is not the only dynamic around conflict that can surface in families. Other dynamics can be where a bull overreacts to conflict only to be met by another bull in the family. This can often lead to a rather loud clash, characterized by emotional fireworks, creating much distress for all involved.

Another dynamic might be one peacemaker being quietly angered and upset at another peacemaker—in other words, eggshell meets eggshell. Both sense the conflict, but do not want to raise the issue for fear of creating distress. Hence, the conflict is like a bad odor in the room that no one acknowledges.

When conflict is mismanaged, as identified in these examples, intimacy and trust are dented and damaged, resulting in lopsided relationships—lopsided in the sense that intimacy is conditional based on the absence of conflict.

THE MANAGER

As the name implies, the manager or values grounded parent approaches conflict by managing the experience, both internally and externally, as opposed to avoiding it or controlling it.

So, what is meant by internally and externally? Internally refers to managing one's "inside world"—emotions, thoughts, and attitude. Externally refers to managing one's "outside world"—their behavior and environment.

In regard to the internal experience, the manager makes focused efforts to handle their stressful feelings in constructive ways by expressing their emotion with respect and self-control. Managers stay attuned to their feelings as well as the emotions of their children and partner. They make efforts to actively listen to, mirror, and validate their child's feelings. They try to take the perspective of others by "walking a mile in their shoes." Managers engage mindfulness to help them stay calm in the midst of an emotional storm.

The manager understands that it is not a matter of IF conflict will happen, but rather WHEN conflict will occur. This type of anticipation helps them to be more mindful and purposeful in how they think about conflict and how to use it to promote learning and growth.

In regard to the external experience, managers behave in keeping with their positive values when addressing conflict. They pay attention to their child's behavior during the conflict, applying clear boundaries and redirecting ungrounded behavior—though not at the expense of invalidating their feelings. Although mindful and sensitive to handling the conflict calmly, the manager does not compromise firmness and authority in the process. This approach is consistent with **authoritative parenting**—one of the four styles of parenting discussed in the chapter on discipline.

In the earlier example, Mr. Jones demonstrated the manager approach to conflict. Knowing that the topic of pornography and healthy sexuality is awkward and uncomfortable, he opted not to avoid it (walk on eggshells) nor did he dominate it by scolding his son and shaming him (bull in China shop). Instead, he engaged his son in a productive conversation around this tough-to-talk-about topic. He remained calm (managing his inside world) while using a respectful tone and words while engaging the conflict (managing the outside world). As a result, this very uncomfortable and easy-to-avoid topic was more manageable for both father and son.

When conflict is managed in families, it creates a culture of balance and healthy intimacy within relationships. Children learn that conflict is part of growing up and that it is important to learn from it. They also learn that even though conflict brings about difficult and

CHAPTER 12: PRODUCTIVE CONFLICT AS A CATALYST FOR GROWTH

strong emotions, their feelings are important and ought to be expressed in values grounded ways. Although it can be unsettling to feel vulnerable in the face of conflict, a culture of respect and dignity promotes healthy engagement and management.

So, how does one become a conflict manager? It starts with being attuned to the various emotions related to conflict. Let's take a moment and do an activity to examine this further.

As highlighted by this activity, conflict brings about many different types of feelings. Since emotions influence much of your behavior, the more aware of or attuned to your feelings you are, the greater your ability to define these often hard-to-define states of the heart.

The more you can define and label your stressful feelings, the less you are defined by them.

ACTIVITY: EMOTIONS AND CONFLICT

- What emotions come along with conflict?
- How are these emotions expressed in your family?
- What would you consider to be healthy ways of showing these feelings? What would you consider to be unhealthy ways?
- How aware are you of your emotions as they relate to conflict?

1	2	3	4	5
Limited Awareness		Moderate Awareness		Very Aware

TWO TYPES OF CONFLICT

Just as there are different kinds of emotions that accompany your experience of conflict, there are also different types of conflict. There is conflict between people and conflict within people. Having worked with many different types, sizes, and shapes of conflict, I have learned over the years that it can be categorized in two general forms: productive conflict and destructive conflict. Below are the definitions of both forms:

> **PRODUCTIVE CONFLICT** consists of a responsive process that is goal- and values-oriented with a positive outcome desired. It is centered on maintaining a shared vision and values that support learning and growth. It involves a process where people attempt to manage the conflict as opposed to controlling it or passively avoiding it.
>
> **DESTRUCTIVE CONFLICT** consists of a reactive process that often is personal and defined by one's stressful circumstances. It involves pride, ego, and is typically handled in a manner focused on the self. The focus is on one's ego, with little, if any, attention given to learning and growth. It involves a process where people attempt to control and dominate the conflict.

Let's look at some examples of both forms. After reading the scenarios below, take a guess at which form of conflict is represented and why.

SCENARIO 1:

Parent: *"Please put your toys away."*

Child: *"But I am not done ... we just built the castle ..."*

CHAPTER 12: PRODUCTIVE CONFLICT AS A CATALYST FOR GROWTH

Parent: "*I said, 'Put your toys away'—NOW!*"

Child: "*But, I don't want to! I wanna play!*" (eyes tearing up)

Parent: "*I am so tired of having to tell you to clean up. Why does it have to be a struggle ALL the time?! Pick them up NOW.*"

Child: "*NO!*"

Parent: "*That's it . . . you're grounded!*"

Which form of conflict is described above? What shows you this?

SCENARIO 2:

Parent: "*You have been on your* (electronic device) *for a while now. It is time to do homework.*"

Preteen: (does not acknowledge parent; continues to look intently at device)

Parent: "*I said, it is time to do your homework. Did you hear me?*"

Preteen: "*Uh-huh.*" (mumbling, he continues to engage with his device)

Parent: "*Okay . . . give me the device. I am tired of always having to remind you to do your homework! You know better . . .*"

Preteen: (sighing, while still looking at the device; has yet to make eye contact with parent) "*STOP CONTROLLING me! I will do it later. Leave me alone.*"

Parent: "*WHAT? Don't tell me what to do . . . you and your attitude . . . I have had enough of it. Hand over the device!*"

Preteen: "*NO! Get away from me!*"

Parent: (Approaches child and attempts to grab the device)

VALUES GROUNDED PARENTING

Preteen: (rolls over and clutches device) *"Leave me alone. I can't stand you. You're always trying to control me. What's your problem?"*

Parent: *"I have had enough of you AND your crappy attitude. GIVE me the device!"*

Which form of conflict is described above? What shows you this?

SCENARIO 3:

Parent: *"You have been on your (electronic device) for a while now. It is time for you to do homework."*

Teen: (does not acknowledge parent; continues to look intently at device)

Parent: (approaches child) *"Please look at me."*

Teen: (continues to engage in device)

Parent: *"Please put the device down and look at me for a minute."*

Teen: (sighs, puts the device down, and looks at parent) *"What? I am in the middle of something."*

Parent: *"Be mindful of your tone as you talk to me. Please put your device on the counter and start your homework."*

Teen: *"Wait—I am not done."*

Parent: *"You know the rules and expectations . . . today is no different."*

Teen: *"A few more minutes . . ."*

CHAPTER 12: PRODUCTIVE CONFLICT AS A CATALYST FOR GROWTH

Parent: "*As we discussed, you need to put your device on the counter now—not in a few minutes.*"

Teen: "*You are trying to CONTROL me! I will do it in a few minutes.*"

Parent: "*I have no desire to control you. As we have discussed, behaving in a responsible manner is part of growing up.*"

Teen: "*I don't wanna do it now. I can do my homework later.*"

Parent: "*I get it . . . doing the right thing is hard to do. I am not asking you to like it . . . rather to do what is tough and what is right.*"

Teen: (Sighs) "*Okay, just a couple more minutes though.*"

Parent: "*I know you can make the right, though tough, decision by putting the device on the counter. Please know that if you choose to avoid your work, you are choosing to lose the privilege of the device for the remainder of the day. I will give you a few seconds to make your decision.*"

Teen: (gets up and puts device on counter)

Which form of conflict is described above? What shows you this?

SCENARIO 4:

Parent: "*Please change your outfit. It is too tight and the shorts are too short. Those clothes are for working out and not for school.*"

Teen: (sighs and gasps) "*Why?*"

Parent: "*Good question. The reason is . . .*"

Teen: (Interrupts parent) "*ALL my friends wear sports bras*"

VALUES GROUNDED PARENTING

Parent: *"Please do not interrupt me. You asked a good question, and I am trying to answer it. The reason has to do with the important values of modesty and dignity. Modesty and dignity are not only revealed in your actions but also your appearance."*

Teen: *"But . . . my friends are good people, and they wear these clothes."*

Parent: *"Indeed . . . your friends are good people . . . and . . . it is important for you to be modest and dignified in how you dress. By doing so, you show others your values and what is valuable about you."*

Teen: *"Really? Do you really think my friends will see me as valuable because of my clothes? I mean . . . I don't make value judgments about the clothes they wear."*

Parent: *"Good question and good point. It is not about judging; it is about how you practice your values and how you invite others to practice positive values as well. This may sound silly to you . . . how you carry yourself, both in your actions and appearance, reveals what is valuable to you. Modesty and dignity are revealed in how we dress and how we act."*

Teen: *"Fine. So you want me to look like a nerd?! My friends will think . . . they will think I am a nerd!"*

Parent: *"Just as you would not want to judge them, I hope they will not judge you. Certainly, they are good friends, and they will accept you and your modest appearance. If not, well, they may need to re-look at the value of friendship."*

Teen: (sighs and walks to room to change)

Which form of conflict is described above? What shows you this?

CHAPTER 12: PRODUCTIVE CONFLICT AS A CATALYST FOR GROWTH

So, as you read through the scenarios, could you see the difference between productive and destructive conflict? Let's look at some of the key differences. Editorial comments (in parentheses) have been added to highlight important points.

SCENARIO 1 (DESTRUCTIVE CONFLICT):

Parent: "*Please put your toys away.*"

(Parent is positive to start. It is recommended to forecast the task to be completed—saying something like "*In two minutes, it will be time to put your toys away.*" Preemptive efforts like forecasting allow the child to process the limit/request and decrease the likelihood of reactivity.)

Child: "*But I am not done . . . we just built the castle . . .*"

(Common response from a child while in their world of play.)

Parent: "I said, 'Put your toys away'—NOW!"

(Parent reacts to the child's response and misses an opportunity to engage in the Validate, Promote, and Consequence approach. Parent could have said something like, "*I see. What a beautiful castle! It looks like you put much effort in building it. It is hard to stop playing, especially when you made such a great castle. It is time, however, to clean up. Please put away your toys neatly.*")

Child: "But, I don't want to! I wanna play!" (eyes tearing up)

(Child reacts to parent's reaction)

Parent: "*I am so tired of having to tell you to clean up. Why does it have to be a struggle ALL the time?! Pick them up—NOW.*"

(The focus has shifted from the value of the task to the

VALUES GROUNDED PARENTING

emotion of the parent. The ego has overshadowed a values grounded opportunity.)

Child: "*NO!*"

Parent: "*That's it. You're grounded!*"

As indicated in the editorial comments, the parent's ego and emotion shifted the focus away from addressing values grounded principles. This can happen so quickly if you are not careful. Consequently, the conflict became personal and both were left feeling upset and empty from the interaction. There was an absence of learning and growth that might have occurred had the parent used the conflict to highlight underlying values and the challenge of trying to consistently practice them.

SCENARIO 2 (DESTRUCTIVE CONFLICT):

Parent: "*You have been on your (electronic device) for a while now. It is time to do homework.*"

(Parent is off to a good start. However, forecasting the task that needs to be completed is recommended.)

Preteen: (does not acknowledge parent; continues to look intently at device)

(Although dismissive, a common response as kids become consumed by their devices)

Parent: "*I said, 'It is time to do your homework.' Did you hear me?*"

(Parent checking back with their child to ensure they heard the request)

Preteen: "*Uh-huh.*" (mumbling, and continues to engage with his device)

CHAPTER 12: PRODUCTIVE CONFLICT AS A CATALYST FOR GROWTH

(Preteen confirms verbally, but nonverbal behavior indicates non-compliance.)

Parent: "*Okay, give me the device. I am tired of always having to remind you to do your homework! You know better . . .*"

(Parent shifts focus from task to their ego and emotion. The conflict is now more about the parent feeling tired and frustrated and less about the child engaging in responsible decision making.)

Preteen: (sighing, while still looking at the device; has yet to make eye contact with parent) "*STOP CONTROLLING me! I will do it later. Leave me alone.*"

(Like the parent, the child personalizes the situation and parent's request. The focus is now personal for both parent and child.)

Parent: "*WHAT? Don't tell me what to do . . . you and your attitude . . . I have had enough of it. Hand over the device!*"

(Frustration and irritation are growing. As a result, a power struggle begins.)

Preteen: "*NO! Get away from me!*"

(Preteen continues to personalize the situation and digs in heels)

Parent: (Approaches child and attempts to grab the device)

(Parent attempts to take physical control)

Preteen: (rolls over and clutches device) "*Leave me alone . . . I can't stand you . . . you're always trying to control me. What's your problem?*"

(It is completely personal now with little or no attention given to the values underlying the situation at hand.)

Parent: "*I have had enough of you AND your crappy attitude. Give me the device!*"

(Parent continues to make it personal, focusing on their emotion and the child's attitude as opposed to the purpose of the request and underlying values)

Preteen: (gets up off the couch, throws the device on the couch, and storms away)

As revealed in the example above, the parent and child make the conflict personal. The parent's ego and stress become the focus while the values and purpose of the conflict go unaddressed. Feeling frustrated and dismissed, the emotion gets the best of both parent and child. Both are left feeling misunderstood by the other and leave the conflict with not only bitterness, but an absence of growth and learning.

SCENARIO 3 (PRODUCTIVE CONFLICT):

Parent: "*You have been on your (electronic device) for a while now. It is time for you to do homework.*"

(Parent is off to a good start. However, forecasting the task that needs to be completed is recommended.)

Teen: (does not acknowledge parent; continues to look intently at device)

Parent: (approaches child) "*Please look at me.*"

(Seeking eye contact communicates the value of the relationship.)

Teen: (continues to engage in device)

CHAPTER 12: PRODUCTIVE CONFLICT AS A CATALYST FOR GROWTH

(Teen is so caught up in electronics that greater focus is put on the device than the relationship.)

Parent: *"Please put the device down and look at me for a minute."*

(Parent respectfully and firmly redirects the focus from device to relationship. Notice how the parent uses behavioral language in identifying desired behaviors (Clarity—one of the five C's).

Teen: (sighs, puts the device down, and looks at parent) *"What? I am in the middle of something."*

(Teen communicates aggravation and frustration with a snarky tone; however, the teen complies with parent's directive.)

Parent: *"Please be mindful of your tone as you talk to me. Please put your device on the counter and start your homework."*

(Parent helps their teen be aware of their tone and redirects focus on behavior—what TO DO.)

Teen: *"Wait . . . I am not done."*

(Teen tests the limits—does the parent really mean what they say and say what they mean?)

Parent: *"You know the rules and expectations . . . today is no different."*

(Rather than engage in a lecture or lengthy monologue, the parent provides a brief reminder. Notice the focus is on the expectations [family blueprint] and NOT on the parent's ego or emotional state.)

Teen: *"A few more minutes . . ."*

(Teen tests the limits again—having difficulty engaging

from what they WANT to do versus what they NEED to do [wants versus needs battle].)

Parent: "*As we discussed, you need to put your device on the counter now—not in a few minutes.*"

(Parent focuses on the first step. Again, rather than begin to lecture, the focus is brief, behavioral, and to the point without using language or a tone that can shift the focus from the task at hand to the parent's ego and emotional state.)

Teen: "*You are trying to CONTROL me! I will do it in a few minutes.*"

(Teen goes from testing the limits to making it personal, which could divert the focus off the task at hand.)

Parent: "*I have no desire to control you. As we have discussed, behaving in a responsible manner is part of growing up. This is the time for you to engage the value of responsibility and do your work.*"

(Parent clarifies the issue of control, inviting ownership. Parent also uses strategy of linking request to the value of responsibility. By introducing the value of responsibility and inviting ownership, the parent declines to make the issue personal and about control.)

Teen: "*I don't wanna do it now . . . I don't like it.*"

(Teen again protests, indicating their focus is more on what they want rather than on what they need to do [wants versus needs battle].)

Parent: "*I get it . . . doing the right thing is hard to do. I am not asking you to like it . . . rather to do what is tough and what is right.*"

CHAPTER 12: PRODUCTIVE CONFLICT AS A CATALYST FOR GROWTH

(Parent validates [part of the VPC approach] their teen's experience and uses a "both/and" approach. Parent communicates an understanding that behaving in values grounded ways is not always easy, and clarifies the value of making active efforts versus avoidance.)

Teen: "*Ugh . . . okay . . . just a couple more minutes though.*"

(Teen attempts one last effort at trying to do what they want versus what they need to do.)

Parent: "*I know you can make the right, though tough, decision by putting the device on the counter. Please know that if you choose to avoid getting your work done, you are choosing to lose the privilege of the device for the remainder of the day. I will give you a few seconds to make your decision.*"

(Parent attempts to positively reinforce [practicing Competency] the right, though tough, decision. Parent also respectfully forecasts the consequence [losing the device for the remainder of the day] to back up the boundary.)

This example illustrates a common conflict over screen use (wants versus needs battle). This scenario highlights the focus is on the parent's shared vision (helping their child grow up) and values and not their ego and emotion. As you follow along their conversation, you can see how maintaining this is key to values grounded parenting. The parent redirects the focus to their relationship and the values, thereby declining any invitation to make it personal and overly emotional. The parent demonstrates understanding that it is tough to be consistent in one's efforts toward being values grounded. Also, note that the parent remains firm and consistent with the boundary.

SCENARIO 4:

Parent: "*Please change your outfit. It is too tight and the shorts are too short. Those clothes are for working out and not for school.*" (Parent redirects child, citing that her outfit is not appropriate for school.)

Teen: (sighs and gasps) "*Why?*"

(Teen tests the limits and questions parent's request.)

Parent: "*Good question. The reason is . . .*"

(Parent attempts to answer question.)

Teen: (interrupts parent) "*ALL my friends wear sports bras*"

(Teen links her question with the context of her friends.)

Parent: "*Please do not interrupt me. You asked a good question, and I am trying to answer it. The reason has to do with important values of modesty and dignity. Modesty and dignity are not only revealed in our actions but also our appearance.*"

(Parent respectfully reminds the teen to listen while keeping the focus on the values underlying the request for her to change her outfit.)

Teen: "*But . . . my friends are good people, and they wear these clothes . . .*"

(Teen begins to personalize the request by indicating that her friends are "good people" irrespective of the clothes they wear.)

Parent: "*Indeed . . . your friends are good people . . . and it is important for you to be modest and dignified in how you dress. By doing so, you show others your values and what is valuable about you.*"

CHAPTER 12: PRODUCTIVE CONFLICT AS A CATALYST FOR GROWTH

(Using a both/and approach, the parent validates the value and goodness of her friends while still maintaining the boundary of the child being values grounded in her appearance.)

Teen: *"Really? Do you really think my friends will see me as valuable because of my clothes? I mean . . . I don't make value judgments about the clothes they wear."*

(Teen challenging how appearance is related to values and introduces the danger of judging others.)

Parent: *"Good question and good point. It is not about judging; it is about how you practice your values and how you invite others to practice positive values as well. This may sound silly to you, but how you carry yourself, both in your actions and appearance, reveals what is valuable to you. Modesty and dignity are revealed in how we dress and how we act."*

(Parent validates teen's concern and question as opposed to taking it as a personal affront. Parent proceeds to keep focus on the values as opposed to making it personal.)

Teen: *"Fine. So you want me to look like a nerd?! My friends will think . . . they will think I am a nerd!"*

(Teen shifts focus back to how others will view her appearance and the insecurities that often come along with this.)

Parent: *"Just as you would not want to judge them, I hope they will not judge you. Certainly, they are good friends, and they will accept you and your modest and dignified values. If not . . . well . . . they may need to re-look at the value of friendship."*

(Parent keeps focus on the values and the importance of how appearance needs to be aligned with such values. Parent also provides some insight on judgment.)

Teen: (sighs, and walks to room to change)

(Teen seems to understand and complies, though she has a different perspective.)

In this scenario, the child presents some abrupt, albeit good questions. The parent maintains the focus on the shared vision and values as opposed to making it personal and about their ego. You can imagine how this conversation would have been different had the parent made it personal. Instead, the parent kept the focus on the values of modesty and dignity, validating the goodness of the child's friends while not supporting the skimpy outfits. The parent used the conflict as an opportunity for dialogue for learning and growth. In the short term, the daughter may not fully grasp the limit, though over time the daughter will understand the relationship between appearance and the values of modesty and dignity.

As the above scenarios illustrate, how you approach and manage conflict greatly influences whether there will be growth, learning, and advancement as an outcome. In the next chapter, the process of using conflict will be broken down into three distinct parts.

SUMMARY AND TAKEAWAYS

- Conflict is natural and occurs within and between people.
- Conflict is part of healthy relationships—not just unhealthy ones.
- Conflict is a catalyst for learning and growth.
    - Conflict moves you and your kids out of your comfort zone where you can experience life from a different perspective.

CHAPTER 12: PRODUCTIVE CONFLICT AS A CATALYST FOR GROWTH

- Using conflict productively promotes growth, learning, and advancement.
- Avoidance or domination of conflict shrinks growth and learning.
- Avoidance or domination of conflict stunts positive intimacy and trust.
- There are generally two types of conflict:
    - Productive: Responsive and collaborative process of working through the conflict, relying on one's values to guide their behavior throughout the process
    - Destructive: Reactive and one-way process that is driven by one's ego and negative emotion where the focus is on control
- There are different approaches to conflict:
    - Walking on eggshells reflects an avoidant approach (destructive)
    - Bull in the China shop reflects attempts to dominate conflict (destructive)
    - The Manager approach attempts to engage the conflict relationally, using a shared vision and positive values to work through the conflict (productive)
    - As a values grounded parent, using the Manager approach you validate the feelings of your children and redirect negative behavior (when necessary).
- Much of the discomfort around conflict comes from the emotions involved.
    - Being emotionally attuned to your feelings and those of your children and partner is key to dealing with the discomfort.

VALUES GROUNDED PARENTING

- ○ The challenge in managing conflict productively is establishing greater comfort with the discomfort.
- ○ It involves handling the stressful feelings in a values grounded manner.

CHAPTER 13

THE THREE E's OF PRODUCTIVE CONFLICT

IN THE PRIOR CHAPTER, the concept of productive conflict was introduced. You learned it is part of any healthy relationship and serves as a catalyst for meaningful learning to occur. When managed productively, conflict strengthens intimacy and trust in your relationships with your children. Given that conflict is part of growing up, managing it productively also protects the integrity of your family culture.

In this chapter, the three stages of productive conflict will be explored. The three stages are: Engagement, Endurance, and Empowerment. As in other chapters, real world examples will be provided to help you see what the concepts look and sound like. Before getting started, it is important to clarify a safety issue. If your physical safety is threatened or others could be harmed, conflict should not be engaged.

ENGAGEMENT

The first stage involves engaging conflict with the intent to *manage* (The Manager Approach) and guide the process so it promotes learning and growth. Oftentimes, it is the first step that can be the most difficult.

CHAPTER 13: THE THREE E'S OF PRODUCTIVE CONFLICT

Many parents and kids feel uncomfortable (upset, aggravated, hurt, dismissed, angry) when conflict is addressed. Yet, if you do not engage it, the discomfort often grows to the point of awkward avoidance and/or emotional overreaction.

So, what does engagement look like? Engagement can be having a difficult conversation with your kids. For instance, initiating conversation on conflict-riddled subjects like wants versus needs, healthy peer relationships (peer pressure), dating, sex/sexuality, happiness versus pleasure, and modest appearance. Another form of engagement involves applying clear, firm limits and negative consequences (in the form of removal of privileges and/or grounding).

When engaging in difficult conversations, it is important to practice the value of humility (one of the 4 Anchor values). By doing so, you acknowledge the challenge in facing the topic/conflict and the uncomfortable emotions that accompany it. This helps validate the discomfort of the experience (mirroring emotion), communicating to your kids that their feelings and perspective are valued. . Here are some examples:

- ☑ "I am not sure how best for us to talk about this, though it is important for us to do so. Let's give it a try and see what happens."
- ☑ "It would be far easier for us to avoid talking about this as it brings up tough-to-deal-with feelings. You are very special to me and worth the effort for us to try to talk about it. Let's try and see what happens."
- ☑ "We are Redivos (family's last name), and that means we do not take the easy way out. Now, with that said, this will be a difficult talk and issue to deal with. Just because it is tough does not mean we avoid or sidestep it. Let's engage it and see how we can use this tough experience to grow."

- ☑ "I understand you are upset with me. It is not my intent to make you upset; rather, it is my intent to help us stay values grounded. Just because this brings up conflict does not mean we should turn our backs on it. Remember, conflict is part of all relationships, ***including ours***. It is important that we find a way to discuss it so we don't buckle in the face of conflict and actually use it to help us grow."
- ☑ "I get that you do not want to talk about it. We don't need to address the conflict this very minute. Let's take some time to think about it first, and before bedtime, let's discuss a plan for dealing with this."

As these examples illustrate, the focus is on being a humble participant in trying to enter a difficult conversation. You may also notice that it is clear from the verbiage that avoidance is not an option. As a leader in your family, it is important to take the first step to engage with your kids. There may be times when you do not **want** to, but will **need** to. ***The wants versus needs battle applies to parents as well!***

Setting limits and disciplining can be another way of engaging in conflict. As mentioned earlier, children can personalize limits and negative consequences, perceiving them as a form of rejection. By anticipating this, you are more prepared for their emotional reaction and hopefully less likely to overreact or avoid as a result. Using the validate, promote, and consequence (VPC) approach along with the 5 C's can help you stay emotionally attuned with your children and consistent with your limits and consequences. Here are some examples:

- ☑ "I can see that you were very frustrated when you yelled at your mom. You had good reason to feel frustrated. You are being grounded not for feeling frustrated, rather for how you expressed your frustration. Calling your mom disrespectful names is not a respectful way to handle your feelings, as stressful as they are."

- ☑ "From what you told me, I can see there was confusion about your homework, specifically what you needed to complete. You lost the privilege of your electronics not because there was confusion about your homework, but because you lied about not having any homework. It is one thing to feel confused; it is another thing to behave in a dishonest way."
- ☑ "If I was in your shoes, I would be very upset and hurt by what your brother said. It is not OK for him to call you names and tease you that way. I will address this with him. You are being grounded not because of feeling angry and hurt, you had good reason to feel that way. Rather, you are being grounded for how you showed your feelings. It is not OK to throw things at him when angry—as you saw, you hit him in the head, causing a cut."

ENDURANCE

The second stage is enduring conflict. Endurance is a reflection of fortitude and perseverance. When you practice endurance in the face of conflict, you are showing your children and family that you are defined by your values and not by snarky and stressful emotion or the challenging circumstances surrounding the conflict.

You are sending an important message to your children and family that you will help lead and guide them to a healthy resolution. This communicates each child is valued. Remember, when you are enduring conflict with one child, the others are watching and studying how you handle it. Without a doubt, they are keeping an eye on whether you will endure the conflict in a values grounded manner.

Using **windshield thinking** can help you endure conflict by shifting your focus to your shared vision. Rather than getting consumed by negative thoughts related to the conflict, look ahead to how you can use the conflict to help your child learn, grow, and advance.

As discussed earlier, your children naturally test the limits in their quest to learn and grow. They grow in all directions, and conflict can provide a useful tool for supporting healthy and positive behavior. By practicing endurance, you are showing your kids that you understand conflict is part of the growing up process and part of balanced and healthy relationships.

In addition to the five C's, it is also helpful to practice the VPC (Validate, Promote, and Consequence) approach. By *validating*, you are affirming the value of your kids' emotions and experience (remember, validating does not mean that you are approving or agreeing with their behavior). You *promote* endurance of the conflict so that the *consequence* will spur meaningful learning and growth.

Let's look at some examples:

- ☑ A preteen who is angry because of being grounded for misuse of electronics

    "I see that you are upset. Being grounded from electronics is tough (validate). My hope is that you understand the purpose behind it (keep focus on purpose). Please deal with this in respectful ways. As a reminder, before the end of your grounding, let's discuss what you learned from this."

CHAPTER 13: THE THREE E'S OF PRODUCTIVE CONFLICT

☑ A teenager who is frustrated and upset because her parents won't let her hang out with a group of friends who are having a negative influence on her.

*"I understand that you feel this boundary is unfair (validate) and want your situation with your friends to be different. Friends are an important part of life **and** it is important to have friends that honor and support positive values. As we discussed, the behavior of this group of friends does not reflect positive values. They seem to be good people who are not making good decisions. Getting in trouble at school shows this. Right now, we may not see eye to eye on this situation, and hopefully we can continue to talk about choosing healthy and positive friends."*

☑ A six-year-old apologizes for hitting his sibling and hopes that his apology might keep him from being grounded.

"Thank you for your apology. I understand that you don't want to hit anymore. I see you are sad and upset about it (validate), and it is my hope that you learn how you can control your behavior (value of self-control) when angry with your brother. It is important for you to learn that you can do this (keep focus on purpose). You will continue to be grounded through the end of the weekend as we discussed earlier."

☑ A nine-year-old being grounded for defiant and disrespectful behavior. After being grounded for this behavior, the child throws a tantrum and makes comments that "these rules suck" and "no one loves me." Rather than engage the child when emotionally escalated, the parent sets an emotional boundary and waits for their child to calm down.

"I could tell you were quite upset about being grounded (validate). As we discussed, your behavior was disrespectful. You are not being grounded for feeling angry, upset, or thinking that the rules stink (separating feelings from behavior). Rather, you are being grounded for yelling bad and disrespectful words and not following the rules. I love you even when you make mistakes (validate), though let's be clear that I do not like your disrespectful and uncooperative behavior (separating behavior from person). Please know that my love for you is much bigger than your mistakes. You made a bad decision. Let's use this conflict to help you grow rather than shrink (engage)."

When showing endurance in the face of conflict, you are shaping your family blueprint in a meaningful way. You help your kids learn that conflict can indeed be productive.

Stressful feelings can represent the growing pains you experience as you endure conflict. As values grounded parents, use endurance to help grow, not shrink, from conflict.

EMPOWERMENT

The third stage is empowerment. This is the stage where you (parent and child) experience and reflect on the personal and relational growth

CHAPTER 13: THE THREE E'S OF PRODUCTIVE CONFLICT

from the conflict. It is the dessert after eating the spinach! You emerge from the conflict feeling stronger and recognizing the positive outcome that comes along with endurance. You have a realization that your relationship endured some challenging circumstances and did not falter or collapse in the face of conflict. As a result, you develop greater self-confidence in navigating and managing conflict.

Empowerment also helps you see that, by engaging and enduring conflict in a values grounded manner, your relationships are more balanced. You and your kids become empowered not only by what you learned from the conflict, but also how you have grown, personally and relationally. You recognize how productive conflict has helped grow your trust and positive intimacy. You are not reliant on the absence of conflict to feel emotionally close.

In the example involving pornography (beginning of Chapter 11), the father and his son were empowered through using a difficult and uncomfortable conversation to address healthy sexuality. By addressing this conflict in a values grounded way, the father opened the door for future conversations on this very important and meaningful topic. This not only strengthened positive intimacy, but it also helped his son learn and grow.

Let's look at some other examples.

In the example below, a parent is talking with their six-year-old child about a conflict involving horseplay while at a grocery store. The parent attempted to redirect the child several times, and the child continued to run around. As a result, the child was grounded for part of the day.

Parent: *"So, let's talk about what happened yesterday. You were pretty upset and we had a conflict. Do you know what I mean by conflict?"*

Child: *"Uh . . . that you were mad at me and I was mad at you."*

VALUES GROUNDED PARENTING

Parent: *"Sort of . . . conflict involves feelings AND it involves us disagreeing about something. In this case, we disagreed on how you should behave in the grocery store."*

Child: *"Do we have to talk about this again?"*

Parent: *"Yes. It is good to talk about what you learned from it. After being told that you were grounded, how did you feel?"*

Child: *"Mad."*

Parent: *"I could tell. How did you show me that you were mad?"*

Child: *"Uh . . . I yelled."*

Parent: *"Yes, and you threw the pillow across the room."*

Child: (*looks down and mumbles "uh–huh"*)

Parent: *"Even though it is hard to do, it is good to talk about this. Please look up at me."*

Child: (*looks up at parent*)

Parent: *"Do you think it is wrong or bad to feel mad?"*

Child: *"Uh-huh" (nodding)*

Parent: *"Actually, it is okay for you to feel mad. I understand that it is upsetting to be grounded. Did you know that it is okay to feel mad?"*

Child: (*shakes his head*)

Parent: *"Well, it is. Your feelings are important. It is your job to show them in good ways . . . ways that are part of our values like respect."*

Child: *"Yeah, but it's not fair that I got grounded when Maria was chasing me."*

CHAPTER 13: THE THREE E'S OF PRODUCTIVE CONFLICT

Parent: *"I see . . . you feel it was unfair. Remember, you were told three times to walk next to the cart and you did not listen. I understand it is tempting to play tag, though you are a first-grader now and fully capable of following directions. Is that correct?"*

Child: *"Uh-huh."*

Parent: *"So, even though you felt it was unfair and you were mad, it is still your job to show your feelings in respectful ways, much like you are doing right now."*

Child: *(smiles)*

Parent: *"You are talking about your feelings in a calm and nice way, and I would say you are showing self-control and respect. Would you agree?"*

Child: *"Uh-huh."*

Parent: *"So, when we have conflict, this is a better, kinder or respectful way of showing and talking about your feelings. Does this make sense?"*

Child: *"Yes."*

Parent: *"Terrific. So, next time when you get mad, how can you show your mad feelings in a respectful way?"*

Child: *"Not yell or throw things . . ."*

Parent: *"Yes . . . so that's what NOT to do. What can you do?"*

Child: *"I don't know."*

Parent: *"Use calm words and self-control. You can also go to your room for a cool-down, or if we are riding in the car, sit on your hands and put your lips together super tight so you keep yourself from yelling and not letting any bad words come out."*

Child: *(smiles) "Can we play now?"*

In the above example, the parent and child process the conflict and feelings. The child revisits the experience, and the parent invites the child to re-examine how the conflict and emotion were managed.

Initially, the child does not want to talk about it, yet the parent assumes leadership and proceeds forward. The parent validates the child's feelings and encourages the child to grow by managing such feelings in respectful ways. Another key takeaway from the above example is the experiential aspect of simply talking about conflict. This normalizes it and makes the subject far more approachable. The parent is guiding the child to develop a voice to discuss, learn, and grow from one's mistakes. The parent does a nice job of positively reinforcing the child's self-control and behavior as they are talking about the conflict. As we can tell from the child's smile, this experience can lead to empowerment.

In this next example, a parent is talking with their teenager about a conflict they endured that involved disrespectful behavior. Specifically, the teen was redirected to disengage from his electronics and complete his homework. The teen reacted by dismissing the parent's request (kept using a device), cursed at the parent, and told the parent "I hate you." As a result, the teen was grounded, including loss of electronics (except for school purposes). As part of the grounding, the teenager was to do a writing assignment centered on managing and expressing anger in positive ways as well as an apology.

> **Parent:** *"I would like for us to talk about the incident that led to your grounding and the conflict we had."*
>
> **Teen:** *"I finished my grounding . . . completed my paper . . . why do we have to talk about it?"*
>
> **Parent:** *"Good question. It is good to talk what you learned from your mistakes."*

CHAPTER 13: THE THREE E'S OF PRODUCTIVE CONFLICT

Teen: *"I learned from it . . . I completed the paper . . . I won't do it again." (sighing)*

Parent: *"That is good to hear that you won't do it again. You did a good job in clarifying expectations of screen use in your paper, and your apology is accepted. How about the way you reacted when asked to do your homework?"*

Teen: *(sheepish smile)*

Parent: *"You also copped quite a negative tone and attitude, using disrespectful words, in addition to saying, 'I hate you.'"*

Teen: *"Well, you made me mad and frustrated. You don't leave me alone . . . like . . . you are trying to control my every move. You just don't understand. You think you know everything when you don't." (sighs)*

Parent: *"I imagine you are right. I don't fully understand and don't know everything. However, using bad words and a disrespectful tone is NOT a respectful nor mature way of showing anger, frustration, and other strong feelings."*

Teen: *"Yeah . . . but it is sooo frustrating sometimes. You just don't get it."*

Parent: *"I bet it is quite frustrating, and I probably will never fully 'get it.' However, using a snarky tone and bad words does not communicate frustration or anger. It communicates disrespect. Can you see that?"*

Teen: *(looks away and to the ceiling, pausing) "Yeah, I see it."*

Parent: *"I don't have an issue if you get upset with me or are frustrated with me. You can tell me directly—like you just did. That is far more mature and respectful than using bad words and saying 'I hate you.'"*

Teen: "*Okay*"

Parent: "*Part of growing up means you need to find and practice respectful ways of handling these tough-to-handle feelings.*"

Teen: "*Yeah . . . I didn't mean to say it; it just . . . slipped out.*"

Parent: "*I understand. Next time, please be more mindful. You can feel frustrated and angry AND behave respectfully at the same time. It's not always easy. It takes strength, and you can do it.*"

Teen: "*Okay, are we done?*"

Parent: "*Yes.*" *(parent gives teen a hug)*

As the above example illustrates, the parent leads the conversation and addresses the issue of their conflict. The parent validates the teen's feelings while not accepting the negative behavior. A central theme is that it's okay to feel frustrated and angry *AND* you can behave respectfully at the same time. The parent acknowledges that expressing strong and stressful feelings in respectful ways is not always easy, yet it is expected that the teen practice. This supports and protects their family culture. The conversation about the conflict serves to empower both parent and teen with takeaways on how to manage conflict productively.

Productive conflict is a key part to maintaining and protecting your family culture, shared vision, and positive values. As you practice it, you are modeling for your kids how to do it.

Conflict is not an easy experience to engage and endure. For most people, it is uncomfortable to varying degrees. *As values grounded parents, it is important to focus on establishing greater comfort with your discomfort* as opposed to wanting the unease and discomfort to disappear. By doing so, you can lead your children through the three stages of productive conflict.

CHAPTER 13: THE THREE E'S OF PRODUCTIVE CONFLICT

SUMMARY AND TAKEAWAYS

- The three E's represent the stages of productive conflict. This structure helps you managed conflict so it becomes a catalyst for meaningful learning and growth.
- Engagement
    - Engage the conflict with your child in a manner that is aligned with your positive values.
    - By engaging and not avoiding conflict, your kids receive the message that conflict is a natural part of all relationships.
    - Taking the first step is often the hardest. Engaging conflict may be having a difficult conversation and/or setting limits and applying negative consequences.
    - Using the VPC approach helps you validate the emotion related to the conflict and promote healthy ways of working through it.
- Endurance
    - This second stage of productive conflict involves enduring the stress and emotion associated with the conflict.
    - You are sending an important message to your children and family that you will help lead and guide them to a healthy resolution.
    - Using the VPC approach helps you stay grounded in your positive values as you manage the conflict.
- Empowerment
    - In this stage, you reflect on the conflict and how it empowered you and your kids to learn and grow.
    - The empowerment stage allows you to see the value of the two earlier stages—engagement and endurance.

- Empowerment allows you to have meaningful conversations with your kids about their takeaways—how the conflict may have helped them learn, grow, and advance.

CHAPTER 14
MISTAKE MAKING AND MISTAKE MANAGEMENT

AS ELUDED TO THROUGHOUT, parenting requires on-the-job learning. This means that mistake making is a regular part of your journey as a parent. Much like conflict, there is a hidden value within mistake making and mistake management.

Mistakes offer your families fertile opportunities to learn and grow. ***Your children simply cannot grow up without making gobs of mistakes.*** As parents, it is important to recognize this and look in the mirror as you remind yourself that everyone messes up in the process of trying to learn and grow.

Parents who acknowledge and try to learn from their mistakes raise children who approach their mess-ups in a similar way. These children and families are more likely to have growth mindsets. On the other hand, parents who do not acknowledge their mistakes can slip into practices of perfectionism. Oftentimes, mistakes are not okay in the eyes of these parents. As a result, their children feel the pressure of perfectionism and tend to avoid taking healthy risks for fear of screwing up.

A friend of mine has struggled with acknowledging her mistakes as well as accepting feedback that could help her grow from them. Not surprisingly, her mother has a similar difficulty. Constructive feedback is often viewed as a personal attack and rejection. Over the years, she and her mother have had conflict regarding this very issue. She has tried to talk with her mother about hurtful experiences she endured as a child. Her mother typically responds in a dismissive way, noting that she did the best she could and had no intention of hurting her. Both are loving people, and neither actively seeks nor intends to be hurtful. However, both are human and have made mistakes that have been hurtful. Perfectionism and pride cloud their ability to see that their mistakes, especially the hurtful ones, can offer valuable learning opportunities to grow personally as well as in their relationships.

As you have heard throughout this book, values grounded parenting is not about being a perfect parent NOR is it about raising mistake-free or perfect children. Rather, values grounded parenting involves actively engaging your mistakes with an interest in learning from them.

In this chapter, mistakes will be explored as a fertilizer from which children and parents can grow and learn. Much like conflict, there is a hidden value within mistakes.

MANURE THEORY OF MISTAKES

"You're late! C'mon, Mike, less go!" my grandpa scolded me in broken English. He was already in his truck, engine running, window down, wearing a harried expression. We were supposed to meet at 5 a.m. and drive over to tend his garden. I looked at my clock, and it read 4:55. In fact, I was five minutes early, but on Grandpa Aldo time, I was ten minutes late. His garden was part of a co-op at a local community college with other green-thumbed weekend growers. On this partic-

ular morning, we had to hurry so we could be the first in line to take advantage of the manure dump. Every month, a huge truck would deliver tons of cow turds.

"*See, Mike, you gotta git it fress. Put it here, and we smooth like tis.*" These were my instructions on what to do with a wheelbarrow load of cow poop. I don't know about you, but a "*fress*" or fresh load of manure at 5:30 in the morning made me want to dry heave.

We worked through the early morning, hauling several loads of manure, tilling the soil, and planting various veggies. It was about 9:30 a.m. and time for lunch. My grandma had packed us a lunch with salami on Italian bread, peppers and onions, chips, and a soda wrapped in tin foil. We lowered his tailgate, sat with our legs dangling, and noshed on our sandwiches. Then, it was back to work.

Whether he knew it or not, Grandpa Aldo was teaching me a key concept within values grounded parenting. He showed me some neighboring gardens, comparing those with and without manure. The difference was remarkable. The gardens with manure had leaves and plants with a vibrant, green hue that was brimming with healthy veggies. The gardens without manure yielded plants that were smaller, less leafy, and not nearly as robust. I thought to myself, *What is it about manure that causes such lively and vigorous growth? Not to be gross, but it is, after all, animal poop!*

As many of you know, manure serves as a natural fertilizer. Although it is counterintuitive to think that animal waste would have rich nutrients to help grow vibrant gardens and lawns, it certainly does. Some of the rich nutrients in manure include phosphorus, potassium, and nitrogen, which turbocharge the soil, making plants not just grow, but thrive. The magic of manure lies in how it strengthens the ground or foundation in which the plants are rooted.

CHAPTER 14: MISTAKE MAKING AND MISTAKE MANAGEMENT

What if you looked at mistakes as a type of developmental manure that helps your kids grow up? What if you used mistakes to help fertilize growth within your children and yourself? What if you viewed mistakes as a means to strengthen your foundation as a family?

After all, there are some striking similarities between the manure used in gardens and the manure from mistakes. Both types of manure stink, and you are tempted to avoid them. Both require a sense of purpose as to why one is choosing to work with something that, at the present time, stinks, but in the long term, will provide positive growth. Both require counterintuitive thinking.

Mistakes and the *stink* that comes along with them elicit feelings of disappointment, discouragement, frustration, and other tough emotions. Yet, at the same time, it is these very mistakes that often provide you with the rich nutrients that help you learn about life and relationships. Mistakes help remind you about using your positive values to work through difficult life challenges.

So, how do you approach mistakes and challenges so you are in a position to learn and grow from them? Let's turn to your shared vision and four Anchor values.

MISTAKE MAKING AND THE FOUR ANCHORS

Your shared vision enables you to rise above your current circumstances (the stress and stink that often come along with mistakes) and see the bigger picture and grander purpose—using the mistake(s) as a growth opportunity. The four Anchor Values help put your vision into action. Practicing *humility* helps open your hearts and minds to recognize you and your kids are imperfect. No matter how old and experienced, you are still learning and growing. Humility enables you to engage and get through the conflict and stress of the mistake. *Accountability* moves you and your kids to a place of accepting responsibility for your mistakes *and* opening yourselves to learn from them. When you practice **gratitude**, you have a sense of clarity and appreciation for how life's challenges and your mistakes help you and your kids learn and grow. Gratitude typically occurs when you look back on your mistakes and lessons learned—not so much at the time. As you attempt to learn and grow from your mistakes and those of others, it is important to be **respectful** in how you and your kids behave in the face of your mess-ups. Practicing respect can be challenging, especially when the mistake is a recycled one, either of your own making or that of your children.

The four Anchor Values work together and help take the shame out of mistakes. Shame is a toxic emotion that can cause you to shrink on the inside, eroding your self-worth. Children who feel shame feel rotten toward themselves. They begin to lose their voice and ability to talk about their mistake. Instead, they begin to talk more about themselves in a shame-based manner. You hear them say things like, "I am a screw-up" and "I am worthless." Rather than being values grounded, they are more ego grounded though with a wounded and damaged ego. For parents who wrestle with shame, the experience can be similar.

You can help protect your family culture from shame by anticipating mistakes and loving your kids (and yourself) through them. In other words, you accept and love the mistake maker (your kids, yourself, or your partner), though not the mistake. This reflects a "both/and" approach to mistakes.

This distinction invites the mistake maker to step up, take accountability for their ungrounded behavior, and work at making behavioral changes to improve. On the other hand, if kids are blamed and shamed for their mistakes, it causes them to hide. They avoid accountability as this is associated with being a bad and rotten person. After all, who

CHAPTER 14: MISTAKE MAKING AND MISTAKE MANAGEMENT

would want to step up, face their mistake, only to be ridiculed and made to feel rotten?

MISTAKE MAKING: SET THE EXAMPLE

As a leader of your family, it is important to set the example and lean into your vulnerability by talking about your mistakes. This can be powerful for your children, and strengthen your family culture. No news flash here; just a simple reminder that your children will follow your example. If you are humble and accountable for your mistakes, they are far more likely to do the same. Let's take a look at an example.

A few years back, I remember trying to "help" my son with his math homework. He was in junior high school and the problems were becoming more complicated and difficult. We sat down together and reviewed several problems in detail. He seemed like he understood and was ready to go. However, he continued to struggle. As most kids do when feeling insecure and unconfident, he began to avoid his worksheet.

In efforts to avoid this frustrating task, he started to look around at other things in the room. Being too focused on completing the task, I completely overlooked his feelings and kept trying to redirect his attention back to the worksheet. My frustration started to build, and I became impatient with his lack of focus and progress.

What did my frustration and impatience look like? I heavily sighed, pursed my lips, and was wringing my hands. Wearing a disappointed expression, I questioned him in a disapproving way, "*what is it you're not understanding?*" My son looked at me with a fearful expression. His focus was no longer on the task, but on my negative feelings. Despite his best efforts, he continued to struggle. I gave myself a time out and then attempted to "help" him a second time. The same outcome repeated itself.

VALUES GROUNDED PARENTING

As you can tell, my impatience and difficulty at managing my frustration ***polluted*** his learning environment. Rather than helping him learn how to isolate variables, my behavior isolated him from the support he needed most. It was not an emotionally safe place for him to learn and grow.

I felt quite sad and guilty for hurting his feelings. My wife helped me see that I needed to be more patient and supportive. Rather than letting things fester, I opted to address my mistake. I apologized to my son (leaning into the four Anchor Values of accountability and humility) and asked for his forgiveness. I clarified that my intent was to help him and not cause him fear. Part of making amends involved me listening to his feelings that I had overlooked. He trusted me again, and shared how he felt. Validating his emotion was important for our relationship. I explained that I will continue to work at listening to his feelings, and practice patience. He smiled, he forgave me, and we hugged. Despite the stink of my mistake, we both learned and grew from it.

My mistake was a humble reminder of staying emotionally attuned with my kids. I also learned how my impatience can get in the way of being a values grounded parent.

To this day, my mistake still serves as a valuable lesson learned. My son still teases me about the hand wringing, and we enjoy a good laugh. This was a victory as I did something for my son that was not done for me when I was a child. The liberation that comes along with humility has been a game changer for me as a father. Please know that mistake managing and mistake management is a lifelong journey. The beauty lies in the voyage, not so much the destination.

How do you approach mistakes in your family? It is important to examine and reflect on this so you can grow as a humble leader within your home. The following activity will help you with this.

CHAPTER 14: MISTAKE MAKING AND MISTAKE MANAGEMENT

> ## ACTIVITY: MESS-UPS AND MISTAKES
>
> 🖉 What is one of your greatest mistakes as a parent and what did you learn from it? How did you grow from it?
>
> 🖉 When you were growing up, how did you and your family handle mistakes? Did you find that you grew or shrunk from your mistakes?
>
> 🖉 What can make it difficult for you to accept your mistakes and talk about them?
>
> 🖉 How can you practice humility and accountability to help your children AND you learn and grow from mistakes?

GROWTH MINDSET

There is a growing body of clinical research and literature about the value of mistake making and learning from it. In her groundbreaking book, *Mindset*, Dr. Carol Dweck (2006) covers this concept within a learning framework. Specifically, she identifies two types of mindsets: Fixed Mindset and Growth Mindset.

People who have a fixed mindset believe their capacity to learn and grow is fixed, based on their level of intelligence, talent, and skill. Because they see these traits as fixed, they tend to reason that effort is not important. People with fixed mindsets tend to avoid challenges as this requires hard work and perseverance. They tend to stay in their comfort zone, and there is a nagging fear of failure in learning new things, especially when effort is involved.

VALUES GROUNDED PARENTING

A fixed mindset can lead to people getting stuck in life. Children and adults who have a fixed mindset are quite hesitant to take on challenging tasks on account that they will make mistakes, and experience failure. They struggle with accepting feedback (a necessary part to working through a tough task) and perceive it as criticism.

A growth mindset, on the other hand, reflects a perception that skill, ability, and talent can and should be developed over time. Since these traits can be strengthened and advanced, those with a growth mindset tend to reason that effort and perseverance are essential to learning and growing. Growth mindset individuals seek challenges based on their belief that they can overcome them, adapt, and grow to be successful. They view feedback as important and essential to improvement. Those with a growth mindset are less fearful of making mistakes and recognize that meaningful growth occurs outside of their comfort zone.

Cultivating a growth mindset within your family culture starts with you, the leader. Encouraging and supporting a growth mindset in your children helps them ***engage, endure***, and eventually become ***empowered*** by the conflict that comes along with mistakes and life challenges.

Here are some practical suggestions on how to introduce, support, and reinforce a growth mindset:

- ☑ Use YouTube videos to introduce the concept of growth mindset.
    - ✓ https://www.youtube.com/watch?v=KUWn_TJTrnU
    - ✓ https://www.youtube.com/watch?v=ivKLEVPI6mM
    - ✓ https://www.youtube.com/watch?v=hiiEeMN7vbQ
- ☑ Search Pinterest and/or Google Free Images for posters and placards on growth mindset. Print out and post in your kids' rooms and bathroom.

CHAPTER 14: MISTAKE MAKING AND MISTAKE MANAGEMENT

- ☑ Do a growth mindset art project as a family.
  - ✓ Create a poster board highlighting the specific practices that support a growth mindset. Hang the poster in your kitchen or family room.
  - ✓ Make a series of sticky-note reminders. Highlight one growth mindset behavior on each note (this supports windshield thinking). Periodically, post the notes on your children's bathroom mirror or in a noticeable place in their bedroom.
- ☑ Create a "mistakes made and lesson learned" marble jar.
  - ✓ Every time your child talks about a mistake they made and the lesson they learned from it, they earn a marble. Your child puts the marble in the jar. Once they reach a certain number of marbles, they earn a treat/reward. This reminds them that there is value in talking about and learning from one's mistakes.
- ☑ During mealtime, discuss growth mindset as a family. Although it may seem a bit awkward at first, this is how culture is built and maintained in our families.

MISTAKES AND GROWING PAINS

As discussed in Chapter 8, growing pains are part of your kids' physical development—a humbling reminder that growth is not always a smooth and pain-free process. Mistakes often bring about emotional growing pains that can cause soreness in your relationships. You may feel them after you mess up as a parent (as reflected in the example of my mistake with my son) and your kids will certainly feel them. It is important to work through your mistakes as a family so that these growing pains don't develop into longstanding wounds.

VALUES GROUNDED PARENTING

One way to keep mistakes from growing into deeper wounds is to address them shortly after they occur in a calm and direct manner. In other words, do not let the pain of mistakes fester. If you do hold on to the pain and keep a grudge, it no longer becomes a growing pain but a wounding one. Apologizing for one's mistake and the pain it caused is an important part of working through it. It is important to practice forgiveness as this helps you move beyond the mistake. Seeking and providing forgiveness not only teaches humility and accountability, but it also helps mend hurts and wounds within relationships. This strengthens positive intimacy in your family.

There are some other proactive ways to address mistake making and mistake management within your family. Here are some practical tips and suggestions:

FAMILY MEETING

As part of a regular family meeting, talk with your children about the value of mistakes and the *hidden nutrients* within these stinky life experiences. Explain that **consequences help them learn from their mistakes.** Since the purpose of consequences is to instruct or teach, their job is to learn from them. Part of this learning process involves them seeking and understanding the lesson learned and using it to help in future decision making about how to behave.

Invite each family member to talk about a mistake, the stink that it caused, and how they grew from it. Take the lead to get the conversation started.

GROWTH CHART

As an art activity, make a Growth Chart with your kids. For ideas, search "growth chart for kids" using Google Images or Pinterest.

CHAPTER 14: MISTAKE MAKING AND MISTAKE MANAGEMENT

Have a section where they can describe their mistake and how it helped them grow. Also include space for various challenging life experiences that they have endured and how these difficult situations have helped them grow.

MISTAKE AND LESSON LEARNED THINK SHEET

As part of boundary/limit setting and grounding, request that your child complete a "Mistake and Lesson Learned Think Sheet." This allows your child an opportunity to reflect on their mistake, what they learned, and how they will approach similar situations differently. Sample worksheets are included in **Appendix D**.

MANURE SCIENCE EXPERIMENT

Do a manure experiment with your kids. Plant some vegetables in separate pots. In some pots, use manure and in others just soil. Be sure to have your kids work with the manure so they experience firsthand the stink that comes along with manure. Compare the growth over time.

POST SIGNS

Search Pinterest or other internet sites for positive images and quotes regarding mistakes and learning. Print out and post on your refrigerator and in your kids' bedrooms.

Remind them that your love for them is much bigger than their mistakes.

MEALTIME CONVERSATIONS

When having a family meal, discuss some of the mistakes you made as a child and parent, and be sure to discuss what you learned from them. Talk about various challenging life situations that you have endured and how you have grown as a result.

DON'T BE THAT PARENT IN THEIR 70s

Imagine that you are older, say in your 70s. It is your grandson's birthday, and you are celebrating with family. During a conversation with one of your kids, they tell you that they wish you would have taken time to be more involved in their lives. Many times, they wanted your advice yet they avoided you out of fear of bothering you and/or worried you would be too disappointed with them about a mistake they had made. What would this be like for you to hear? How would you feel on the inside?

This regretful situation can easily be avoided by simply asking for regular feedback from your kids. During a ride in the car or another captive time (such as mealtime), ask your kids for feedback on how you are doing as a parent. For instance, you can ask, "I would like some feedback on how I am doing as your mom/dad." How many of you had a parent that deliberately sought your feedback? I imagine not many—yet it is a tremendous gift.

What might stand in your way of seeking feedback from your kids? Pride can certainly be a barrier as well as a fear of being vulnerable. A good number of parents believe that they ought to know most if not all the answers. This belief is unfortunate as parenting, no matter how many children you have raised, involves on-the-job learning and growing.

The reality is that leading your kids is tough and confusing at times. Your leadership journey is rife with mistakes. If pride overshadows your humility, you can easily find yourself as that 70-year-old parent who chose not to seek, accept, and integrate feedback.

TWO FOR THE PRICE OF ONE

Effective leaders provide vision, direction, support, *and* routinely seek feedback from those they are leading. As a values grounded parent, you lead your kids and also seek their feedback. In so doing, you get two for the price of one. You not only get valuable feedback on how you can

CHAPTER 14: MISTAKE MAKING AND MISTAKE MANAGEMENT

better parent, but you are also modeling the humility and openness to feedback you want your children to practice (Growth Mindset). It is one thing to tell your kids they need to accept feedback; it is a whole different experience when you model this for them.

Why is feedback so important? Because without it, you can easily stall and become stuck as a parent, spouse, and person. Feedback opens up different perspectives for you to consider, engage, and integrate to improve as a parent. After all, there is a reason why this valuable experience is termed feedback—it *feeds* you information about how you can become better at what you do. **Feedback is the food or fuel underlying your growth.**

ACCEPTING VERSUS LIKING

Let's quickly differentiate between the experience of accepting feedback and the experience of liking it. Many times the food or fuel inside the *feed*back does not taste particularly good. However, what is healthiest is not always the most desirable.

Receiving and accepting feedback takes practice. When giving feedback to your kids, especially teens, do not be discouraged if they respond with a foul expression, grunts, snarls, and growls. Just because your kids don't like the feedback does not mean it is unhealthy. Same goes for you as a parent. Feedback from your kids can sting or hit an "ego nerve" causing an emotional jolt inside you. Rather than become defensive, challenge yourself to listen, even if you disagree at first. Next, process the feedback in a calm and mindful way before responding. When you are mindful, you set the tone for your kids to practice the same approach.

When providing feedback to your kids, use respectful words and a humble approach. This helps create a safe place for your kids to listen and process. Allow some time for your kids to process and then check back to see what their takeaways were from your feedback. Remember to stay emotionally attuned to them as they attempt to process your feedback.

DON'T BITE THE HAND THAT FEEDS YOU

Asking for feedback not only puts you in a vulnerable position, but also your kids. In sharing feedback with you, your **kids take a risk—they risk you getting upset at them and dismissing their feedback.** When they share, try to do these three things in this order: Listen, Listen, and Listen! It is good practice to paraphrase back to them what you heard. Model humility and mindfulness for them as they share their valuable feedback.

Let's remember that this feedback represents food or fuel for your growth. If you become defensive, they are far less likely to offer feedback in the future. *In other words, do not bite the hand that feeds you!*

SUMMARY AND TAKEAWAYS

- Mistakes are an important part of the learning process for children *and* parents.
- Just like manure, mistakes can bring along a stink that can make them hard to deal with.
    - The stink of mistakes is often reflected in strain in your relationships along with stressful feelings, like disappointment, frustration, sadness, confusion, helplessness, and anger.
    - Using strategies from productive conflict can help you work through the stink of mistakes so you can learn and grow from them.
- Practicing a growth mindset helps you use mistakes as fertilizer for growth.

CHAPTER 14: MISTAKE MAKING AND MISTAKE MANAGEMENT

- Accepting and integrating feedback helps fuel a growth mindset.
- Love and accept the mistake maker and not the mistake.
- Practicing the four Anchor Values helps take the shame out of mistakes.
- Consistently discussing mistakes and lessons learned as well as other engaging family activities supports windshield thinking on using mistakes to grow, learn, and thrive.

APPENDIX A
SHARED VISION SAMPLES

These can also be saved as screen savers on your phone and computer.

THE REDIVOS' SHARED VISION

To raise our children with love and to help them grow up, learn, and thrive by consistently modeling our positive values every day.

Our Shared Vision will guide our decision making as parents.

Mike Redivo _____ Date _____

Anne Redivo _____ Date _____

APPENDIX A: SHARED VISION SAMPLES

ORTIZ SHARED VISION

To teach our kids the importance of family and love, and the values to be strong and responsible adults.

Our Shared Vision will guide our decision making as parents.

Carlos Ortiz _____ Date _____

Juanita Ortiz _____ Date _____

WILLIAMS SHARED VISION

To love our children through teaching positive values and treating others how they wish to be treated (Golden Rule)

Our Shared Vision will guide our decision making as parents.

Cody Williams _____ Date _____

Sophia Williams _____ Date _____

APPENDIX B

REFERENCE GUIDE OF PRACTICAL STRATEGIES AND TIPS FOR APPLYING BOUNDARIES, LIMITS, AND CONSEQUENCES

THE FOLLOWING REFERENCE GUIDE provides a review of key tips and strategies on using boundaries, limits, and consequences.

- ☑ Stay calm and mindful when setting boundaries. Calmness helps you be clear and more objective in addressing limit-testing behavior.
- ☑ Remember your children are children—they are not small adults. They will make mistakes and test limits in their process of learning and growing.
- ☑ Remember, children often experience boundaries, limits, and negative consequences as a form of rejection.
    - ✓ Anticipate an emotional response.
    - ✓ Encourage your children to express such emotion in a values grounded way, for example, expressing anger in respectful ways.

APPENDIX B: REFERENCE GUIDE

- ✓ Make eye contact and use a calm, yet focused tone.
- ✓ Focus your redirection toward positive/prosocial behaviors you want them to practice.
- ✓ Tell them what you want them TO DO versus what NOT to do.
  - ☒ "Talk in a calm voice" versus "Stop shouting"
  - ☒ "Keep hands to self" versus "Don't poke your brother"
  - ☒ "Pick up your toys and put them away" versus "Don't leave a mess"
- ☑ Use behavioral language versus an emotional language.
  - ✓ "Please use respectful words" versus "That was RUDE!"
  - ✓ "Please lower your voice" versus "You will NOT talk TO ME THAT WAY!"
  - ✓ "Please keep your hands to yourself" versus "That's enough . . . you're driving your sister crazy!"
- ☑ Be brief and to the point. Keep it simple, clarifying expectations versus over-talking.
  - ✓ "Sit quietly"
  - ✓ "Hands to self"
  - ✓ "Use respectful words"
- ☑ Be pre-emptive and forecast what will happen. Explain what is going to happen before it happens.
  - ✓ "In five minutes, we will pack up and leave the park."
  - ✓ (On the way home from school) "Remember the routine when you get home. You get a snack, have a 30-minute rest-and-relax period, and then your homework needs to be completed."
  - ✓ "Before we go into the grocery store, let's review the

VALUES GROUNDED PARENTING

two key rules: 1. If you see something you would like, write it down and we can discuss it when we get home; 2. Walk calmly and talk quietly—the store is not a playground."

- ☑ Regularly clarify your family blueprint and write the expectations down and post them.
    - ✓ Use **Linking** to align your expectations to your family culture and values.
    - ✓ Be proactive and review expectations regularly.
- ☑ Focus your efforts on managing/controlling your behavior versus controlling your child's behavior.
- ☑ Rather than trying to MAKE your child stop yelling, focus your efforts on keeping a calm and firm voice yourself. Use consequences to back up your limits and teach.
- ☑ Focus on a four-to-one ratio—four positive consequences for every one negative consequence.
- ☑ Be behavioral in your language.
- ☑ Avoid power struggles by declining to get involved in arguments or trying to one-up your child. Take the personal out and keep the focus on maintaining your shared vision/purpose as a parent and positive values.
- ☑ Make limits and boundaries about behavior and NOT the person, for example, "your behavior is bad" as opposed to "you are a bad child."
- ☑ Use limits and boundaries to redirect behavior and NOT emotion. Emotion is neither right nor wrong, whereas behavior can be right or wrong, for example, "It is okay to feel angry, though it is not appropriate to yell and use foul language."
- ☑ Apply consequences shortly after observing behavior.

APPENDIX B: REFERENCE GUIDE

- ☑ Have frequent reminders of the following:
  - ✓ Children will test limits in their efforts to learn and grow. It is my job to set clear, consistent, and firm limits to help my kids learn.
  - ✓ Limit and boundary testing is not about me or my ego. It is about my child's need for feedback in their process of learning and growing.
  - ✓ Limits and boundaries are NOT designed to keep my kids from stressing me out. It is my job to manage my stress. Limits and boundaries are about supporting and protecting my kids' efforts at growing up in a healthy and positive direction.
- ☑ Allow your children to experience the emotional consequences related to their behavior.
  - ✓ Set an emotional boundary between you and your children.
  - ✓ Avoid taking on your child's emotion. This makes negative consequences far less personal.
- ☑ Refer to the section on calmness and know your "stress buttons."
  - ✓ Avoid posing "Why" questions to your kids, such as:
  - ✓ "*Why* do I have to constantly repeat myself five times before you listen?"
  - ✓ "I have already told you 'NO.' *Why* do you keep asking?"
  - ✓ "*Why* do you make things so difficult?!"

APPENDIX C
BEHAVIOR CONTRACT FOR TECHNOLOGY USE

BEHAVIOR CONTRACT FOR TECHNOLOGY USE

This contract applies to the use of the following types of screens/technology:

1. _____

2. _____

3. _____

4. _____

5. _____

APPENDIX C: BEHAVIOR CONTRACT FOR TECHNOLOGY USE

Use of technology is a privilege and not my right. I will practice gratitude for this privilege.

I agree that my screen time will consist of the following:

Weekdays: _____

Weekends: _____

- ☐ These daily times are set and not negotiable. There will be no banking of time from one day to the next.
- ☐ Homework and other values grounded responsibilities need to be completed before use of screens.
- ☐ Use of screens to do homework will only involve that activity. There will be no gaming or social media use.
- ☐ I will not share any personal information if I am allowed to play online games. This includes phone numbers, names, home address, email address, passwords, date of birth, as well as _____.
- ☐ When told to disconnect from the screens, I will practice respectful behavior in doing so.
- ☐ I will provide all passwords of my programs and screens to my parents.
- ☐ I understand and agree that my parents can check my usage of screens at any time. I will be willing to show them things like history, emails, texts, posts, and _____.

- ☐ I will demonstrate respect and integrity in how I use my screens. This means I will use respectful language and respectful images/photos, search appropriate websites, and _____,
- ☐ If someone contacts me that I do not know and/or if I feel uncomfortable with an exchange with a friend or contact, I will notify my parents.
- ☐ I will answer my parents' phone calls, emails, texts, or _____. If I miss a call, I will return it immediately.
- ☐ I agree to be screen free at school, work, family activities, mealtime, and _____.
- ☐ All screens (including cell phones) are to be put in the kitchen or _____ 30 minutes before bedtime.

I am grateful to have the use of technology and will not abuse this privilege. I agree to follow the terms of this contract. If I violate any part of the contract, I fully understand and agree that I will lose the privilege of screen use for a period of time to be determined by my parents.

Signature Child: _____ Date: _____

Signature Parents: _____ Date: _____

APPENDIX D
MISTAKE AND LESSON LEARNED THINK SHEETS

Child Version: This form is designed for elementary-aged children (ages six through ten)

MISTAKE AND LESSON LEARNED SHEET

Name: _____ Date: _____

Describe the mistake you made (How was my behavior a problem?)	
How did my behavior affect others?	
What value or values do I need to practice? (How will practicing these values help me grow up?)	
What did I learn from my mistake? What will I do different next time?	

Depending on ability and age, it is recommended that parents work on this form with younger children and those who need assistance (either with writing or understanding the questions).

Be sure to apologize and say you're sorry to those effected by your mistake. This helps you and others move forward from your mistakes.

_____   _____
Signed   Parent

APPENDIX D: MISTAKE AND LESSON LEARNED THINK SHEET

Mistake and Lesson Learned Think Sheet for
Middle School–Aged Children

This form is designed for junior high–aged children
(ages 11 through 14)

MISTAKE AND LESSON LEARNED SHEET

1. Describe the problem or conflict. What mistake did you make in handling the problem?

_____
_____
_____

2. How did your behavior effect others?

_____
_____
_____

3. What value or values do you need to practice more?

_____
_____
_____

4. Wants versus Needs Battle. Was the mistake related to doing what you wanted versus needed to do? Explain.

_____
_____
_____

5. Describe what you learned from your mistake. How will you use this lesson to help you mature and grow up?

_____
_____
_____

Be sure to apologize for your mistake so you can move forward beyond your mistake.

APPENDIX D: MISTAKE AND LESSON LEARNED THINK SHEET

Mistake and Lesson Learned Think Sheet for High School–Aged Children

This form is designed for high-school teens (ages 14 through 18)

MISTAKE AND LESSON LEARNED SHEET

1. Describe the problem or conflict. What mistake did you make in handling the problem?

_____
_____
_____

2. How did your behavior affect others?

_____
_____
_____

3. What value or values do you need to practice more?

_____
_____
_____

4. Wants versus Needs Battle. Was the mistake related to doing what you wanted versus needed to do? How does doing what you want versus need impact your maturity?

_____
_____
_____

5. Describe what you learned from your mistake. How will you use this lesson to help you improve and mature into the young adult you seek to be?

_____
_____
_____

Be sure to apologize for your mistake so you can move forward beyond your mistake.

ACKNOWLEDGMENTS

WRITING THIS SECTION IS THE FUN PART of being an author. There is much I have learned throughout this journey. Most days I found myself reflecting on the multitude of people, their stories and lived experiences that embody the beauty and challenge of parenthood. With much gratitude and appreciation, I would like to acknowledge and thank the following people.

First, I would like to thank my parents. To my mom . . . you showed me how to love and be a loving parent. You encouraged me to follow my passion and dreams, and see the positive in people. Through your kindness, patience, and gentleness, you taught me much about the values of compassion, optimism, faith, perseverance, and joy. I miss you and your delicious chocolate chip cookies! To my dad . . . you showed me how to stay strong in the face of adversity, the importance of character, and a solid work ethic. You have been there for me at crucial times in my career. It is through your love and words of support that I was able to take on and endure many of life's challenges.

To Aunt Mary . . . you helped me believe in myself when I faced strong headwinds of doubt. During graduate school, your

ACKNOWLEDGMENTS

cards and kind and consistent support helped me stay the course. I don't think this book would be written had I opted to leave school. You and Mom helped me see the power of resilience and overcoming life's obstacles.

I would like to thank my graduate school professors who took the time and care to teach a very green 20-something-year-old student, especially Drs. Peter Chang and Ed Bourg. I have much gratitude to Milciades Morales, a.k.a. "Mil," my first clinical supervisor. You nudged me out of my comfort zone and taught me the value of taking appropriate risks so I could grow and learn. You modeled having a growth mindset before it was ever defined!

To Drs. Delane Kinney and Rudy Buckman . . . thank you for grounding me and helping me loosen up from taking myself so seriously. Your kind mentorship along with the team at Salesmanship Club helped me embrace and celebrate diversity and what is good and positive in people.

To the many client families, parents, children, and students who gave me the privilege to work, learn, and grow with them over the years . . . I am indebted to you for helping me see the power of family and the strong love that fuels parenthood. I am grateful for how you helped me grow both professionally and personally.

To the Desert Heights Academy team . . . your spirit and faith in being values grounded in serving our students was amazing and uplifting. Your tireless work in helping students made the Values Grounded approach come to life—your work truly captured something much bigger than any of us or all of us combined. You helped me see the power of vision and purpose and its value in helping guide children, teens, and adults to learn, grow, and thrive. I especially want to thank my good friend Sam Wright, a.k.a. Mr. Wright, for supporting and encouraging the evolution of the Values Grounded ideas and concepts. You helped put the "productive" in productive conflict.

To my colleagues and friends who supported the Values Grounded approach and encouraged me to introduce it to others. There are too many to mention here, but know that I think of you and am grateful for our valued work together in shaping and influencing the minds of parents, educators, and mental health professionals.

To my good friends who offered words of encouragement and support. In particular, thank you Jason Devlin for your curiosity, interest, and feedback while noshing on some wings and beer. Bruce, thank you for your fellowship and being that friend who helped me deepen my relationship with our loving God. As we discussed, the values grounded model comes from above. To my brother Tim, who is also my best friend . . . thank you for your unconditional support, encouragement, and prayer.

Thanks be to God for his grace and sharing His spirit with me to write this book. The concepts are yours—I am grateful and humble that you prompted me to take on this task (despite my grumbling in the early stages). This has been a wonderful experience and I am grateful that I have grown closer with You along the way. May You bless the parents (and their families) who read this book.

To my editor Vicki Adang . . . your clarity and guidance made this challenging experience an exciting adventure. Your feedback made this book come alive.

Finally, thank you to my beautiful family . . . you are my light. Marcello and Amelie, you taught me parenting AND life lessons that no book, theory, or class could ever come close to. I am grateful for your love, patience, forgiveness, and silliness. It has been a tremendous blessing to have the opportunity to be your dad and share in your process of

ACKNOWLEDGMENTS

growing up. You have inspired my life. To my beautiful wife, Annemarie ... thank you for being a terrific and loving mom to our beautiful kids and sharing in our parenthood journey. Through you, I have learned faith, perseverance, balance, and the fruits of the Holy Spirit. Thank you for sharing your creativity and helping with the book cover.

REFERENCES

Dweck, C. S. (2006). *Mindset: the new psychology of success.* New York: Ballantine Books.

Emmons, R. A., & McCullough, M. (2012). *The Psychology of Gratitude.* Oxford University Press.

Keng, S., Smoski, M.J., Robins, CJ (2011). "Effects of Mindfulness on Psychological Health: A Review of Empirical Studies." *Clinical Psychology Review,* 6, 1041–1056.

Piaget, J. (1936). *Origins of intelligence in the child.* London: Routledge & Kegan Paul.

Weil, A. (1999). *Breathing: The master key to self healing.* Sounds True Audiobooks.

ABOUT THE AUTHOR

DR. MICHAEL REDIVO, a licensed clinical psychologist, has extensive experience in working with parents, families, children, and organizations. Throughout his career, he has served in several leadership roles, including executive director of a private school for children and teens with emotional and behavioral issues. Dr. Redivo has provided training and consultation for parent groups, school districts, private schools, and business organizations. Through this work, he has empowered families, school districts, and organizations to grow and transform their culture to embody values grounded principles. Additionally, Dr. Redivo has served as director of clinical training for doctoral and post-doctoral students in psychology, providing supervision and oversight to emerging professionals. The most rewarding and meaningful role he has served is being a dad. He lives in Arizona, with his wife and children.

LETTER TO READERS

THANK YOU FOR YOUR SUPPORT in buying and reading this book. The vision of *Values Grounded Parenting* is to help families create a strong culture within their home. It serves to empower families to ground their identity within hearty and solid values and not be defined by the broader culture nor their day-to-day circumstances.

In addition to helping families transform their culture, the Values Grounded model helps organizations and school districts cultivate a healthy foundation designed to accomplish their mission and vision. It helps grow values within the staff and those whom the organization serves. Please visit the website at www.valuesgrounded.com and check out additional program opportunities, including videos, training, consultation, and speaking engagements.

Please take a brief moment to provide a review of this book. Your review is not only helpful feedback for me, but it also informs other parents seeking useful books and resources. I am in the process of writing other related books, and your feedback will help guide this process.

Thank you again for your interest and feedback.

Stay Grounded!
Michael

www.ingramcontent.com/pod-product-compliance
Lightning Source LLC
Chambersburg PA
CBHW031059080526
44587CB00011B/746